TROMPE L'OEIL
MURALS using stencils

Melanie Royals

NORTH LIGHT BOOKS
CINCINNATI, OHIO
www.nlbooks.com

ABOUT THE AUTHOR

Melanie Royals is a self-taught artist who, since 1984, has been exploring
and discovering the endless possibilities and artistic applications inherent
in the art of stenciling. An intense love of the combination of color,
pattern and design, combined with a keen sense of style and decoration and
a desire to share it, led to the release of the Royal Design Studio stencil
line in 1994. A nationally renowned innovator and educator in the decorative
painting field, Melanie now shares her love and knowledge of stencil art
through instructional videos, magazine articles, books and television
appearances. Additionally, Melanie personally shares her signature techniques
and style through workshops held at the school she founded in 1996, The San
Diego School of Decorative Arts, as well as in special appearances at fine
decorative painting institutions nationwide.

Trompe L'oeil Murals Using Stencils. © 2000 by Melanie Royals. Manufactured in China. All rights reserved. The patterns and drawings
in this book are for the personal use of the artist. By permission of author and publisher, they may either be hand-traced or photocopied to
make single copies, but under no circumstances may they be resold or republished. No other part of this book may be reproduced in any
form or by any electronic or mechanical means including information storage and retrieval systems without permission in writing from the
publisher, except by a reviewer, who may quote brief passages in a review. Published by North Light Books, an imprint of F&W Publications,
Inc., 4700 East Galbraith Road, Cincinnati, Ohio, 45236. (800) 289-0963. First edition.

06 05 04 03 02   9 8 7 6 5

Library of Congress Cataloging-in-Publication Data
Royals, Melanie.
    Trompe l'oeil murals using stencils / by Melanie Royals.
            p.   cm.
    Includes index.
    ISBN 1-58180-028-2
    1. Stencil work. 2. Trompe l'oeil painting. 3. Mural painting and decoration. I. Title: Trompe l'oeil murals using stencils. II. Title.
TT270 .R68 2001
751.7'3–dc21
                                                                    00-041824

Editor: Jane Friedman
Designer: Wendy Dunning
Production artist: Kathy Gardner
Production coordinator: John Peavler
Photographer: Larry Stanley

DEDICATION

I dedicate this book to my son, Daniel, a true work of art who makes me proud every day.

ACKNOWLEDGMENTS

It would not have been possible for me to have gotten through the creation of this book without the help and patience—and extreme flexibility—of my photographer, Larry Stanley. His willingness to work around my crazy schedule and within my time frame, all with a great sense of humor (and love of fly specking), as well as his fabulous photography, went above and beyond any of my expectations.

Thank you to Jean Louis-Corradi for his assistance, love and support throughout the creative and painting process.

Thank you to Marcelino da Silva for taking time out of a busy schedule to create the step-by-step sequence for the *faux bois*.

A special thank you to Richard and Andrea Tober for coming in under the wire (in the late night and early morning hours) with their perspective on perspective, and to Richard especially for creating the step-by-step illustrations and patterns.

Thank you to my editor, Jane Friedman, for her patience and calm as deadlines came and went, time and again.

Thank you to the stencil designers who so graciously contributed stencils for use in this book: Deesigns, L.A. Stencilworks, The Mad Stencilist, Muracles by Jeff Raum, Nature's Vignettes, P.J.'s Decorative Stencils, Red Lion Stencils, and to Peggy Eisenberg of Decorative Accents for her artistic contribution to the gallery.

A very special thank you to the staff of Royal Design Studio, most especially Jan Petek, who keep the business running while I "play" with paint!

And finally, thank you to my grandmother, Dorothy Chestnut, for passing on to me her artistic talents and devotion to decorative painting.

TABLE OF CONTENTS

INTRODUCTION

Trompe l'oeil, a painting technique that involves the use of visual devices and tricks that are designed to literally "fool the eye" of the viewer and (for an instant) make him believe that he is seeing something real and dimensional, has been practiced by artists for centuries.

This art form has been used through the ages to adorn churches, castles and the homes of nobility. Most often, it was used to represent classical forms in architecture, such as moldings, bas-relief, columns and capitals. The effective use of light and shadow combined with texture and a believable perspective (point of view) create the illusion of a three-dimensional object or mural on a two-dimensional surface.

The use of trompe l'oeil painting reached its peak during the Renaissance. Changes in taste led to a gradual decline in its use. Impressionistic and contemporary art, which gained momentum in the late nineteenth and early twentieth centuries, represented objects in more non-specific ways.

All things being cyclical, trompe l'oeil painting has enjoyed a resurgence of late, along with other forms of decorative painting and art. It is seen extensively today in commercial applica-

LEFT
This trompe l'oeil mural was created with stencils from Royal Design Studio. The flagstone stencil is from Nature's Vignettes. What looks to be an incredible amount of painted work is actually very simple and easy to execute by simply using the edge of the stencil to develop the shading and contrasting values that create the illusion of a three-dimensional surface.

tions and in public art, as well as in homes both stately and simple.

In addition to a renewed appreciation for decorative art, there is growing interest among artists and nonartists to develop painting skills that will enable them to create their own masterpieces using trompe l'oeil and decorative painting.

This book focuses on skills and tech-

niques that can be learned, used and adapted by anyone with an interest in developing her artistic talents. Whether you plan to use them in your own home or as a professional, whether you are a skilled artist already or you have never taken pencil to paper or paint to a wall, you will find the inspiration, instruction and encouragement here to transform ordinary surfaces into artistic illusions. Learning freehand painting skills and mastering proper brush and blending techniques can take years of

study and practice! Fortunately, you have a variety of tools at your disposal that can simplify the application of your great ideas and creativity to transform surfaces in your environment into works of art.

In fact, if you are prone to call yourself a nonartist, and find yourself saying, "But I can't draw or paint," then this book is definitely for you! Through the use of stencils, shields and tape, the creation of trompe l'oeil illusions becomes easy and accessible to potential artists of all skill levels. We will take the basic concepts of using simple tools to control and limit the application of paint and use them to define space, create three-dimensional looks easily and develop the shadows and highlights that make painted illusions come to life.

My goal with this book is to give you the basic information, simple techniques and tools that will allow you to easily develop the skills that will enable you to

• create believable textures with painted effects

• utilize correct perspective and define space

• visually represent the values and contrast necessary to create the illusion and dimension and trompe l'oeil art

These three things—texture, perspective and value contrast—done correctly will lend realism and polish to your painting, whatever your skill level.

By combining these techniques with the rules of layout and composition, architectural elements and simple decorative painting treatments, we will create *trompe l'oeil murals*!

chapter one

STENCILS

One of the most versatile and useful tools available to artists is the stencil. Stencils have been used as a tool to create surface decoration for thousands of years and have many unique qualities. A stencil, in its simplest form, is nothing more than a shape that is cut out of a semirigid surface. When the shape is in the form of a specific design and paint is applied through it to a hard surface, a print is made.

It is the complexity of the stencil design and the technique that is used to apply the paint that determines what the finished result will look like. A heavy, uniform application of paint through a simple, single-overlay stencil design will result in a very graphic or primitive look. Using a multiple-overlay stencil design with a studied approach to color application and careful attention to creating contrast and detailed shading will result in a print that appears sophisticated, dimensional and hand-painted.

The basic concept behind the use of stencils, and what makes them so unique and useful to artists (and potential artists) like us, is that they control and limit the application of paint on a surface. The uncut areas of the stencil form a barrier between the paint and the surface. The paint is limited only to those areas that are cut out and exposed. When we use the edges of the cutout areas to build up layers of paint and shading, a dimensional look results. We will extend that concept—the controlled and limited application of paint—to our use of shields and tape as well. Once you start working with this concept, you will undoubtedly begin to find and develop your own applications

for these marvelous tools as you realize what time-savers they are!

Artists employ a variety of techniques and materials for stenciling. We will examine all our options here and when each might be most useful for our trompe l'oeil mural work. Please remember: there is no right way, and the "no rules" rule rules! In the fifteen years I've been stenciling, I have definitely developed my own shortcuts, techniques and

preferences (and I'm very happy to share them). You will develop your own favorite techniques and preferences as well. You will find the most success with using and perfecting techniques with mediums that are comfortable for you at your own taste and skill level. We'll discuss those options shortly. First, though, let's start with some useful tools and supplies you will need.

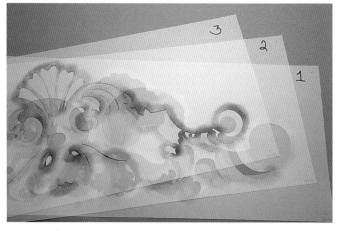

Multi-overlay designs are stenciled one after the other. Each piece contains separate elements of the design that interlock, much like a jigsaw puzzle, to form the whole design.

The use of a multi-overlay stencil allows you to work with contrasting values, building up areas of both dark values and lighter highlights, which creates a realistic dimensional look. Notice that because there are no bridges or unpainted areas, it is difficult to tell that a stencil has been used at all when viewing the completed design.

A solid application of paint through a simple but beautiful design produces a look that is very graphic and mechanical, similar to block printing or silk screening.

Tools and Supplies

STENCIL BRUSHES

The quality of your work will depend greatly on the quality of your tools and materials, and no tools are more important than the brushes you use. Natural-hair brushes with long, soft bristles will yield the best results for the stencil method that is featured in this book. Short, stiff-bristled brushes will not only make it hard to achieve the soft, blended effect that a firm, swirling motion produces, they will be hard on your wrist and arm as well!

Brushes come in a wide variety of sizes, from ¼" (6mm) up to 1½" (4cm). The size of brush you use will depend on the size of the area you are stenciling. For large open areas, such as pots or sizable architectural elements, you will want a larger brush that fills in the space quickly. Using a small brush will take longer, and you will most likely end up with a blotchy, uneven effect.

FOAM STENCIL ROLLERS

A dense foam roller is another option for stenciling large areas that don't require varied depth of color, such as large architectural elements. Foam rollers allow you to cover a lot of ground quickly and are indispensable for large mural work. Where necessary, additional shading can also be added with a stencil brush after the roller work is complete.

Here's a selection of stencil brushes.

Use a foam roller to quickly fill in a large area.

TAPES AND ADHESIVES

Blue tape. Most professionals use blue painter's tape. It is more expensive than masking tape but retains its tack much longer (so it can be used repeatedly). It also has less of a tendency to harm or remove paint from the work surface when pulled off.

Easy Mask paper tape. This tape resembles a Post-it Note and is sticky on just one edge. It allows for straight, clean lines on a smooth surface and is ideal for creating and building architectural elements. Like the blue tape, it also can be used repeatedly.

Other tapes. For masking off curved areas, use thin masking or pinstriping tape. These will flex easily enough to protect curved areas, such as elongated leaves, and to create arches and rounded objects.

Repositionable stencil adhesive spray. For large stencils and weak stencils (meaning that a large portion of the material is cut away) and for any situation in which you desire a more secure seal, spray adhesive can be very useful. Lay your stencil right side down on newsprint or scrap paper and lightly mist with adhesive. Hold the can at least 12" (30cm) away from the surface and don't overapply. Allow the adhesive to dry briefly before pressing the stencil onto the surface. The stencil may be moved and used repeatedly before reapplying adhesive.

ADHESIVE HINT

After you have sprayed your stencils, be very careful not to let them fold up on themselves. When two surfaces with adhesive meet, they will create a strong bond, and you will have a mess on (in) your hands.

An assortment of tape includes from left to right, $\frac{1}{4}$" masking tape, Easy Mask paper tape and blue painter's tape.

Repositionable spray adhesive provides a secure seal.

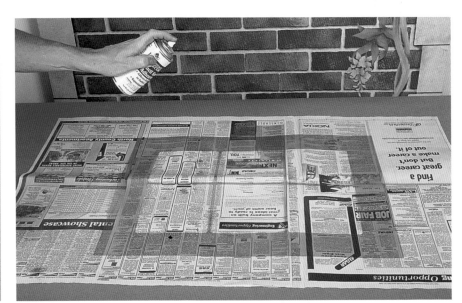

Hold the spray adhesive approximately 12" (30cm) away from the stencil as you apply a light misting.

PAPER TOWELS

I highly encourage all of my students to use Bounty paper towels or something similar of high quality. The primary purpose of the paper towels is to remove almost all of the paint from your brushes after you load them by "off-loading" with a hard pressure, so the towels need to be strong and absorbent. Another purpose of off-loading is to be sure that your paint is distributed evenly on the brush to produce an even print. Lower-quality towels will not take enough paint off the brush and will shred under the pressure.

CONTAINERS

Small plastic cups work well for keeping colors separated and for keeping thinned paint in one place. They are available at restaurant supply stores in a variety of sizes.

You're thinking either I'm insane or those paper towel people are paying me off! No, neither, but after many years of practicing and teaching stenciling, I've found that the most important step to achieving a wonderfully blended, soft stencil print is to properly off-load the brush on very good quality paper towels, and Bounty fits the bill every time. Bounty paper towels are shown on the left and some bargain brand on the right. No bargain there. Save them for drying your hands!

Small plastic cups are handy for keeping thinned paint separated. To keep extra paint from drying out, use plastic lids or store in airtight containers.

MEASURING AND MARKING TOOLS

Measuring up to the job requires tools for creating straight and level lines. Here are some items you will find very useful for stenciled mural work.

Pencils and artist's erasers. Use soft lead pencils and keep marks and lines light so they are easy to erase and to paint over.

Watercolor pencils. A damp cloth or sponge easily removes watercolor pencils, or they dissolve and blend in with the paint. Choose a light color when drawing or marking over a dark background, and a light, neutral color (such as soft gray) for a light background.

Bubble level. Levels are mandatory tools to be used when creating or "building" architectural elements. Use them to mark truly level (horizontal) lines and perfectly plumb (vertical) lines.

Chalk line. When laying out long lines, use a chalk line. Pull the line taught between two predetermined points and snap it by pulling slightly away from the surface and letting go. The chalk on the line will transfer to the surface. An alternative to using colored chalk (especially when marking dark surfaces) is using baby powder, which doesn't leave any residue or color your painting.

Clear grid ruler. I find clear grid rulers indispensable for all kinds of measuring and marking. You can easily draw right angles and parallel lines by lining up the grid lines on the transparent ruler.

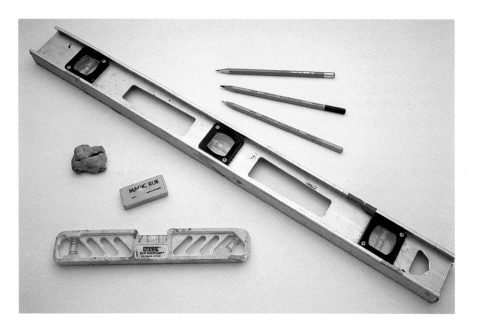

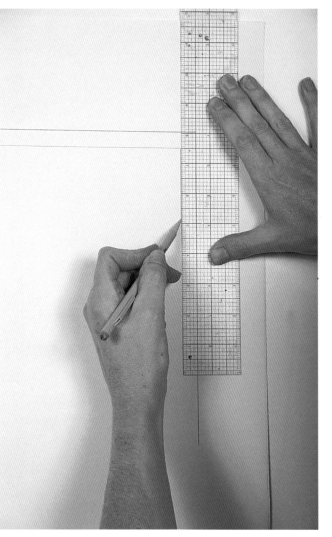

Use a transparent grid ruler for quick, accurate measurements. You can easily create parallel lines by lining up the first line with the measurement on the ruler that is the thickness you desire, then drawing the second line along the edge of the ruler.

Paint Mediums

ACRYLIC PAINT

The majority of the projects and techniques in this book call for craft acrylic paints. These offer many advantages: They are readily available in a wide range of premixed colors. With the addition of water or FolkArt Extender they can be made translucent to create a glazelike or watercolor effect. Unthinned, they can be used opaque and will cover previous colors well. They dry quickly, so multiple coats and colors can be layered quickly without muddying.

EXTENDER

For creating soft, blended, translucent effects, and for making acrylics easier to paint with, we will be adding FolkArt Extender to the acrylic paint. Undiluted, acrylic paint is very heavy and builds up quickly and excessively on both stencils and brushes, making it difficult to stencil effectively. The addition of extender completely changes these properties, making the paint flow easier for softer, blended prints. It also makes cleanup of stencils and brushes much easier—*a big plus!*

OIL-BASED STENCIL PAINT

Many artists prefer to work with stencil cremes, which are oil-based paints in a solid, cakelike form. These are available both as crayons and in pots. Many beginning stencil artists find these very easy to work with because they naturally produce a soft effect beginning artists find it easy to control the buildup of paint. The disadvantages for mural work are that the cremes come in a limited color range, don't layer well (because they are not opaque and they muddy when multiple colors are used together) and do not completely dry for days.

Because they do stay soft and blend easily, I have found them to be most useful for creating softly gradated shadows and architectural elements with tape. Because you are putting on such a thin layer of paint, it is possible to paint over these with water-based paints, so you can feel free to mix both mediums in mural work.

The addition of extender to ordinary craft acrylics creates an entirely different medium that is ideal for trompe l'oeil stenciling because it allows for easy shading and color blending.

Paint cremes allow for easy shading and blending and work wonderfully for creating shadows.

LATEX PAINT

Latex paints can be used for stenciling in large areas and creating architectural elements such as columns and block walls. Latex paint builds up very quickly on the stencil, is tacky and is hard to clean, so it is definitely not recommended for intricate designs. It does not dry as quickly as acrylic paint, so you will have to wait a bit between building up coats of paint. Latex paints can be thinned and made more translucent by adding water and glazing mediums.

GLAZE

Waterbased glazing mediums can be added to latex paint to make it more translucent and easier to work with. We will be using glazes and a variety of manipulative tools to create trompe l'oeil surface textures on our stenciled elements.

PAINT FOR EXTERIOR SURFACES

For painting murals on exterior surfaces, several companies have developed lines of waterbased paints that will bond to concrete, terra cotta and stucco, and will not fade, peel or crack under adverse weather conditions and strong sunlight.

Latex paints are extremely useful and cost-effective when your stenciling and painting will cover large areas. I recommend using a flat finish in a 100 percent acrylic, exterior grade.

Just a little glaze medium added to latex paint will make it more suitable for brush stenciling. A larger ratio of glaze to paint will create a translucent medium that can be manipulated with tools over large areas to produce a variety of effects. Note: The more glaze that is added, the "wetter" the medium becomes, and longer drying and curing times will be required.

Two good lines of paints that are widely available and created specifically for painting outdoors are Plaid's Durable Colors and Patio Paints from DecoArt.

Cleaning Brushes and Stencils

STENCIL BRUSHES

Stencil brushes are sturdy little guys and will last many years with some basic care. The most important things to remember: Do not allow paint to dry in the brush. Brushes are much more sensitive when wet, so be sure they are not pressing up against something as they are drying or they will dry with a permanent bend. Be sure the brush is completely dry before attempting to stencil with it again.

Take care of brushes by cleaning well after each use and you will find that they last for years. I like to keep handy a brush soak container, filled with a mixture of one part concentrated Murphy Oil Soap and two parts water. As I finish with a particular color and brush, I drop it in to soak until I am ready to clean up at the end of the day.

For oil-based cleanup, work out as much excess oil-based paint as possible on paper towels. If you are going to reuse the brush soon, paper towel cleanup should be sufficient. Otherwise, clean brushes with Murphy Oil Soap and water, or rub across paper towels that have a few drops of baby oil on them.

Follow up by working out all paint with a good brush cleaner. A small plastic brush scrubber will get in between bristles to easily remove traces of paint. The paint may stain the bristles and leave them slightly colored, but you will know when you have removed all traces because the water will run clear.

STENCILS

I am pretty fanatical about cleaning stencils. Stencils with layers of paint built up on them are harder to work with. The dried paint creates more drag on the brush. Additionally, the paint will build in on the stencil, throwing the registration off on multi-overlay designs. Without proper cleaning, you will lose the benefit of the translucency of the plastic, which allows you to see previous prints and more easily line up subsequent overlays.

Stencils cut from Mylar should last through many uses and years with some care. The amount of elbow grease that will go into cleaning them will depend on the paint medium used.

Acrylic and latex paints that have been thinned with either extender or glaze will clean up easily with warm water and a kitchen scrubber sponge.

Spray on a little cleaner, such as Murphy Oil Soap, Simple Green or Formula 409, for even easier cleanup.

If you are using oil-based paint cremes, clean your stencils immediately after use by simply wiping with a clean paper towel. If you've allowed the paint to dry and cure you will need to use mineral spirits and a little pressure to get your stencils clean.

For thick, dried paint, you may want to let your stencils soak. Lay out a plastic garbage bag and layer stencils with healthy squirts of any of the above cleaners. Fold up completely in the plastic and allow to sit for several hours to overnight. The paint should almost slide off at this point.

When cleaning stencils, always take care not to bend back pointy areas or tear at delicate bridges. Stencils should be allowed to lie flat for cleaning, so if it is a very large stencil, you will need to put it in the bathtub. You may or may not want to clean the tub while you're there!

Inadvertent tears in the stencil can be fixed by placing clear tape over the damaged seam on both sides. Carefully cut any excess tape away from the edges with a sharp craft knife.

Stenciling Techniques

The stencil is simply a tool that is used to easily define the shape and form of the design by allowing paint only into limited areas. It is the techniques used by the artist while stenciling, (color selection, shading, highlighting, value contrast, etc.) that will bring the design to life and give it dimension and realism. Stenciling techniques are easy to learn and master; all that is required is some good, basic instruction, quality tools and practice, practice, practice!

STENCILING 101

Always hold the brush perpendicular (straight up and down) to the surface while stenciling, and while loading and off-loading the paint.

To properly off-load the brush, rub with a very firm circular motion on paper towels. The size of paint circles that you make should be at least twice the diameter of the stencil brush. This ensures that you are removing excess paint as well as distributing paint evenly on the brush.

Keep this concept in mind: You are building up thin, translucent layers of color. It is much better to apply two thin layers of paint than one thick one. If you try to build up too much color too quickly, paint may seep under your stencil.

Each time you reload the brush, you are beginning again with more paint, so lessen your pressure on the brush to avoid starting too dark.

Adding extender will make your paint more translucent. If you need your paint color to cover or hide something that has been painted underneath, or just wish to create a more solid effect, don't add extender.

If you want even more opacity to the color, add some white to it.

If you can see brush marks in your print, you have too much paint on the brush. A sufficiently dry brush allows you to place nice, firm pressure on the brush, which will give you a soft, smooth, completely blended effect.

The most common mistake made is leaving too much paint on the brush. When you are beginning and getting a feel for it, take off more paint than you think necessary. You can always add more layers and build up more color.

It is the amount of pressure placed on the brush that affects the depth of color on the print. A good warm-up practice (shown below) is to load the brush and do a value study. Start with a firm but light pressure to create a soft blush of color. Then, without reloading your brush, increase your pressure (this comes through the shoulder) to create a medium value. Finally, press very hard to create a dark solid value. Now go back to the light pressure again, trying to feel the difference.

As a rule, it is hard for most people to believe what a small amount of paint is necessary for stenciling. If you are unsure about how much paint on the brush is too much, here's a simple test: Lightly brush across the back of your hand with the loaded stencil brush. If you see paint there, you have too much!

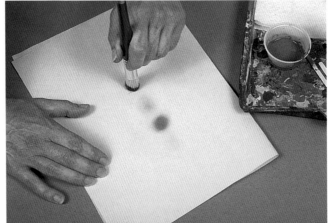

Making a value study

SWIRLING

Swirling is the stenciling technique I prefer because it produces a softly blended, refined, hand-painted look. With some practice, you will find that it is very easy to achieve the shaded, dimensional look that is essential to trompe l'oeil painting. Simply concentrate paint along the edges of the stencil and control the amount of pressure you are putting on the brush. More pressure, more paint.

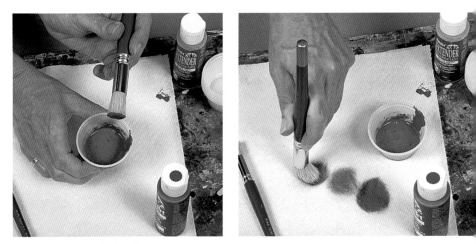

1 *Correctly load the brush*
For a translucent effect and easier shading, thin paint with FolkArt Extender to the consistency of melted ice cream, generally a few drops of extender per teaspoon of paint. Stir well. Load just the tip of the brush by dipping straight into the stencil paint, and remove excess by rubbing in a firm circular motion on the paper towels. I have found that most students do not press hard enough or off-load enough paint at first because they can't believe that you can treat a brush that way. They also think that they need more paint on the brush than they actually do! A good technique for off-loading is to create three circles of paint that become progressively lighter. Also notice the circles of paint are more than twice the diameter of the brush. This means you are pressing firmly enough to remove the correct amount of paint.

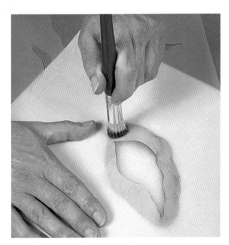

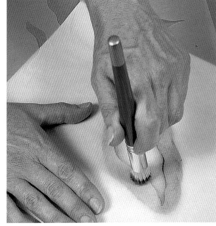

2 *The stenciling technique*
Begin stenciling by first concentrating paint around the edges of the cutout areas of the design, constantly moving the brush in small, firm circles as you continue around the outer portion of the exposed areas of the design. Notice that the majority of the stencil brush is on the Mylar at this point. This serves to define the edge of the design cleanly and clearly with a deeper color that naturally fades away in value toward the center. I like to push the brush into the edge to achieve a nice clean, crisp edge. Remember to build up color slowly! You can always go back and add more.

3 *Filling in*
Gradually blend in the color toward the middle of the exposed area by using a lighter pressure and a dryer brush. The fade out of color should be gradual, not abrupt. This will take some practice as you learn to adjust your pressure.

4 *The completed print*
By using a very dry brush held perpendicular to the surface, and maintaining a nice even pressure while building up translucent color, I was able to create this soft, powdery print with a dimensional look.

STIPPLING

Stippling, which is sometimes referred to as pouncing, is an alternative brush-stroke used for applying paint through the stencil. A stippled print has a more textural, grainy quality to it. Stippling deposits and builds up the paint more quickly and heavily, so it is useful when you are trying to cover over a background color or trying to bring back a lighter color over a darker one, as in the creation of highlights.

Stippling is a straight up-and-down, tapping motion with the brush. Because you are not pushing into the edges of the stencil as in the dry-brush method, you may leave a little more paint on the brush. If your brush is too heavily loaded with paint, you can still experience some seepage under the stencil, so don't forget to off-load paint!

STENCILING WITH ROLLERS

When you want to cover a large area quickly and evenly, roller stenciling is the way to go. It is very important to still work dry, so that you don't have excess paint seeping under the edges. A light misting with spray adhesive will help hold the edges of large stencils securely. A firm, even pressure with the roller will give a smoother look. As always, it is best to build up the paint slowly, and two (or more) thin layers with nice clean edges are better that one thick sloppy one. Note: It is important to allow the first layer of paint to dry completely before adding additional coats. It the paint underneath is still slightly wet, you will lift that layer off as you try to apply more paint onto it.

For quick even coverage, use a stencil roller. Keep in mind that you are still working dry, and off-load excess paint on absorbent paper towels or clean newsprint. Just as with a brush, it is important to have the paint distributed evenly on the roller. In a situation where you are going for a uniform look, start from the center and work out to the edges. This way, you are removing more excess paint from the roller before you work toward the edges.

STENCILING WITH OIL-BASED PAINT CREMES

Cremes are excellent for creating very soft, blended looks because they stay wet. This allows you to go back and rework areas, softening and blending them further. You can even remove excess buildup of paint by rubbing gently with a paper towel. Cremes come in a limited color range and can't be pre-mixed, so you must create new colors by blending two or three colors together as you work. This allows for a very painterly look, with the colors blending easily into each other. The downside to this is that you can't layer colors without them blending and muddying, because they don't dry instantly on the surface like acrylics do.

The technique for stenciling with cremes is similar to that of using extended acrylics, however, you will load the brush a little differently.

1 Load and off-load the brush
Load the brush by rubbing directly into the paint. Remember that a little goes a long way. You can always come back and get more paint if you need it. It is not necessary to off-load excess color to nearly the extent that using acrylics requires. I do like to make sure that the paint is blended evenly on the brush, however, and always rub a little circle first on paper towels or a portion of the Mylar. Off-loading the excess on the mylar allows you to go back and pick up additional paint from there as you need it.

2 Work from the outside in
Just as with the swirling technique done with acrylics, you will want to develop the color slowly. Begin by working the color around the edges of the design, and then blend toward the center, adjusting your pressure as you go.

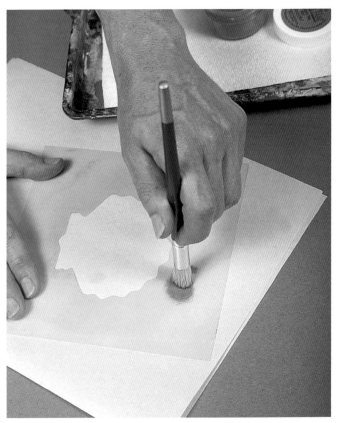

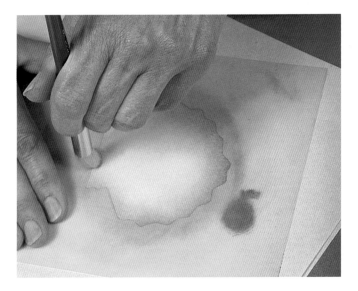

3 Paint Creme Considerations

Because the paint does not dry completely right away you will want to be careful of paint on your hands and excess paint on the Mylar that could be messy. If you are using a dry brush and not depositing excessive amounts of paint on the surface, your print will be dry enough to immediately place another overlay on top of it without worry. If you want to flip your stencil over to get the mirror image, you will need to clean it off first to avoid transferring paint to places you don't want it.

PROOFING YOUR STENCILS

I always recommend to my students to stencil practice proofs on newsprint. It is inexpensive and easy to get and will give you a wonderful surface to stencil on. Whenever you are working with a new, unfamiliar design, it will be to your benefit to play around with it a bit. Try out various color combinations and techniques. Study how the elements of the design relate to each other to determine how to shade properly and effectively. Use your proofs to determine where you will position those elements in your mural and to see how they relate to the rest of the composition and your design space.

Other good materials for stenciling proofs are frosted Mylar and acetate, especially when you are planning free-form designs and murals. The paint adheres and blends well on the frosted side of the material, and you then have a translucent proof that you can place over previously painted areas and see how the new elements will fit in. You can even flip the proof over to see the reverse effect.

Use stenciled proofs to determine color selections and shading patterns. You then will have a useful tool for planning positioning of elements in your mural.

chapter two

TROMPE L'OEIL STENCILING

Now that you are familiar with the basic tools and techniques that are inherent to the art of stenciling, we will focus on some more-detailed techniques that go beyond merely filling in the blanks and allow us to create true trompe l'oeil: the painted illusion of a three-dimensional object on a flat, two-dimensional surface.

What is it that separates trompe l'oeil stenciling from ordinary stenciling? With trompe l'oeil stenciling we are not simply creating pretty patterns; we are focusing on realistic-looking objects and architectural features. As with any type of trompe l'oeil work, we will concentrate on four important basic elements. The first element involves establishing a well-defined light source and shading appropriately. We will also focus on creating surface textures that correspond to the object we are trying to represent (this aspect will be demonstrated in chapter four). Developing contrasting values is the third element. This contrast in values will occur between the object and background, and within elements of the object itself. Contrasting values draw the viewer into the illusion and help define spatial relationships. It defines where one element ends and another one begins. Value contrasts can be subtle or very sharp and well defined, depending on the desired effect and the quality of light being represented. Lastly, we will concentrate on using shading and highlighting correctly to effectively create and model the effect of a three-dimensional form. Shading tells the viewer what shape the object takes, which areas come forward and which recede, and also where the object sits in relationship to the light source.

This trompe l'oeil mural combines stencil elements from Royal Design Studio, The Mad Stencilist and Muracles by Jeff Raum. Note the effective use of a well-defined light source and the differences in the variety of surface textures on the objects themselves. Also notice how the shading and highlights follow and conform to the shape of the objects and how contrasts in values help to separate and define space. The velvet drapery will be seen again on page 84 as a step-by-step technique.

You can see the effect that shading and highlighting have on these stenciled, basic shapes: A circle becomes a sphere, a rectangle becomes a column, a triangle becomes a cone and a square becomes a raised panel. By reversing the application of light and shadow, we can create an entirely different illusion—that of a concave, rather that convex, surface.

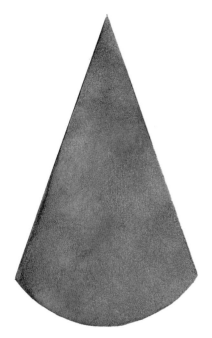

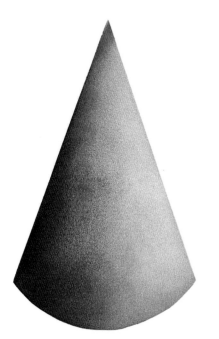

Successful Theorem Stenciling

The term theorem stenciling originally referred to the 18th-century art of painting on light-colored cotton velvet that was taught to young women as a "polite occupation," along with other types of painting and handiwork. The theorems most commonly took the form of still-life paintings: realistic bowls and baskets filled with fruits, and floral motifs. They were executed with oil paints in bright, vivid colors and embellished with hand-painting.

This style of painting is also sometimes referred to as bridgeless, or multi-overlay, stenciling. The process involves using a series of overlays (separate pieces of Mylar) to complete the print. Each overlay has different elements of the design cut into it with spaces in between so that the elements are separated from each other by areas of uncut Mylar. This allows you to shade and color each portion of the design individually.

When the overlays are precisely cut, you should be able to stencil them one after the other, with the elements of the design fitting together snugly, like pieces of a jigsaw puzzle. With proper shading, the result is more of a hand-painted look than a stenciled one because you do not see unpainted areas or lines between the painted portions that are present in single-overlay stencils.

ONE STEP AT A TIME

Theorem stenciling is done in layers. Each layer, or overlay, contains only portions of the completed design. As each overlay is completed, the design begins to develop as the elements lock in and come together.

The first time you work with a new stencil design, the various cutout portions will just look like a series of odd shapes. At this point, you don't know where you want shading and highlight-ing because it is impossible to see how each element relates to the others. The best approach I've found is to go through and stencil each overlay lightly at first. Once the whole design is in place you can study it to determine how to shade correctly. Note: Many precut stencil designs for trompe l'oeil work come with detailed instructions and pictures of finished examples that you can refer to. Also, be aware that once you become more familiar with a design through use and practice, the painting and shading process becomes much quicker.

The following demonstration uses a two-overlay leaf design. This group of leaves is part of a free-form set of leaves that can be used and combined with some simple hand-painting to create the tree featured in the mural on page 6.

These fleur-de-lis designs demonstrate how effective multi-overlay stencils are at creating a hand-painted look. While the stencil on the left has a decidedly stenciled look to it, the stencil on the right looks carved and dimensional, thanks to proper shading and an absence of tell-tale bridges.

1 Position the first overlay. If there are pinpoint registration marks, you will transfer them lightly at this point using a soft lead pencil. If you want to avoid marking your surface, you can place small pieces of tape underneath the Mylar and mark the registration points directly on the tape. This allows you to make nice dark marks that are removed along with the tape. Stencil using the dry-brush method, building up color along the edges of the design and fade toward the middle. Keep your color light at this point, because you want to give yourself somewhere to go, valuewise, with your shading later.

2 Align the second overlay using the registration marks. There is an even more important place for your registration to match up, however, and that is where the edges of the elements meet. Each piece fits into the next, similar to a jigsaw puzzle. You should not be able to see anything you have previously stenciled showing through the exposed areas, because what you will stencil now will lie right next to it. This means that it is important to have well-defined edges of stenciling. Don't allow your edges to fade out. This photograph shows the second overlay positioned correctly. Laser-cut stencils are highly accurate, and there is one spot where the whole design locks into place. Move the stencil around slightly until you can see that all of the connecting edges of the design match up.

This photograph shows misalignment, which should be apparent because there are portions of previous stenciling visible. This will cause overlapping in some places and gaps in others.

3 Once the design is based in with color, replace the stencil overlays one at a time and go back and add more depth and dimension with deeper shading. Study the layering of the leaves. Some are in front and fully visible, and some are partially obscured by other leaves. The areas where the overlapping occurs need to be visually separated by creating contrast. If everything is painted in the same value, the look remains flat.

4 Contrast in values causes the eye to see some elements as coming forward and others receding. The lighter values will naturally appear to come forward, while the darker areas will seem to recede.

FIXING GAPS IN YOUR STENCILING

Without proper alignment and registration, you will end up with unpainted gaps between the stenciled areas. Like anything else you do with paint, they can be fixed. Simply nudge the stencil over to accommodate the error, and fill in with paint. It is best to do this repair work on the side that will be getting darker shading anyway, so that you don't end up building up additional color in an area you wanted to leave lighter.

TOP LEFT

The darker shading will occur on areas where they appear to go behind elements that are overlapping them. This is an interpretation of how light affects how we view an object. Darkness occurs in the absence of light, so where the light would be blocked from hitting an object by something that is shielding it, it will be darker. Where an object is getting unobstructed light, it will be lighter.

TOP RIGHT

In the case of this leaf grouping, some of the leaves are meant to appear as if they are curled up in front of themselves. The portion that is curled up in front will be lighter, but note how I have shaded along the edge where it curves back away from view to soften it and give it a rounded effect.

Here's the completed shading.

VISUAL LAYERING: TROMPE L'OEIL POT PROJECT

Visual layering is key to creating successful illusions with stencils. When you begin working with a stencil, the outline of the exact design is already there in your hand. The design has been drawn, and someone has determined how to divide it into the individual pieces and overlays that will create a whole image. You must bring that image to life and make sense of it. You must study the individual parts and determine how they relate to the whole. From there you must determine the correct way to shade to show depth.

This project will expand further on how to use shading and contrast to define form and space. As the artist who gets to make the decision, I have determined that the primary light source is coming from the upper right.

WHAT YOU'LL NEED

- Large Acanthus Leaf Pot stencil from Royal Design Studio
- FolkArt Acrylics: Burnt Umber, Cappucino, Tapioca and Terra Cotta
- FolkArt Extender
- 1" (3cm), ½" (1cm) and ⅜" (1cm) stencil brushes
- blue tape

1 Base-paint the pot
As with the stenciling of the group of leaves, I have gone through with a 1" (3cm) brush and lightly base-painted the design with Cappucino so that I am now able to study it to determine how the various parts should be represented in relationship to each other and to my point of view. At this point, you can differentiate between the various elements of the design, but the lack of contrast in values leaves it looking flat. Once you are familiar and comfortable with a design, this base-painting step may be eliminated and you can shade as you go.

2 Carefully reposition overlays
Theorem stencils are generally not cut so that one overlay contains all of the highlighted elements and another contains all of the shaded elements. Sometimes that works and sometimes it doesn't, depending on the design. In this case I have carefully repositioned the first overlay back where it originally was, using tape to hold it in place. I want it to be secure but have the ability to lift it back to study each element individually. I am now ready to use shading and highlighting to create more dimension by visually pushing back some areas by increasing the shading and contrast and pulling others forward by either leaving them lighter or actually adding a lighter highlighting color to them.

3 Establish middle values
It is always best to start light and build up layers of color slowly. It is very easy to go back and add just a touch more color, and you want to leave yourself someplace to go with your values. With Terra Cotta and a ½" (1cm) brush, use a light touch to begin separating and defining the different elements by adding deeper shading.

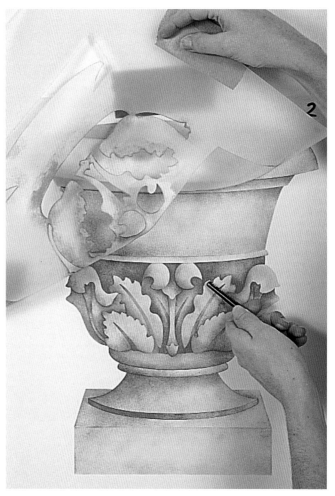

4 Shade in relation to form and light source

As you start to add the shading that will sculpt and model the form, you will need to be constantly aware of two things: the light source and the push-pull effect. How you shade an element will be affected by both of those factors. An element may be rounded and protruding forward. If it is in the direct line of the light, you will be shading deeper on the side that is opposite of the light, but also using lighter shading to create the illusion of roundness on the highlight side. Another factor to consider as you work is color value. If an element is in front of or on top of other elements, you will want to leave the value lighter where it comes in front. When the behind element is given a contrasting darker value, it will recede, and the illusion will be successful. In this case I am using my deepest shading color, Burnt Umber, with a smaller ⅜" (1cm) brush. The smaller brush size allows for better control of the color in tighter areas.

5 Create sharp contrast to make the image "pop"

Your viewer's eyes will be drawn to the areas of greatest contrast. To create a sharper, crisper contrast, add darker darks and lighter lights using more Burnt Umber and Tapioca respectively with the ⅜" (1cm) brush. These accent colors need to be added selectively and do not simply repeat previous shading. Reserve these colors for the deepest recessed areas for the dark shading and those areas in the most direct line of the light for the highlights.

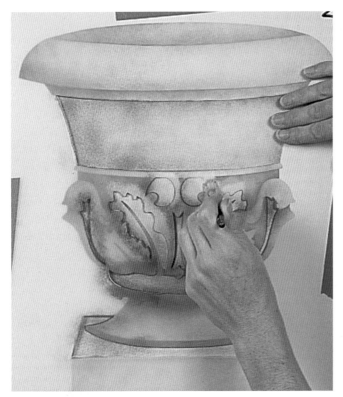

6 Highlight

Stipple on a lighter highlight color (Tapioca) on the areas of the object that would receive the most direct light. Use the ⅜" (1cm) brush and concentrate the color just along the edge of the stencil.

SHADING AND HIGHLIGHTING: NOT A BLACK-AND-WHITE ISSUE

Many beginning or untrained artists commonly and mistakenly paint deep shadows as black. While this would certainly provide a lot of contrast and pop, it is incorrect. The colors of shadows and highlights are always affected by the surface they appear on. They do not obliterate it, and they are transparent, not opaque.

For this reason, we will be using transparent, thinned colors for shading and highlighting. The dry brush stenciling technique lends itself very well toward helping to create a transparent effect, since the color is generally applied in thin transparent layers anyway, allowing the background color to reflect through it.

The Completed Pot

The finished project uses strong contrasts and accents, which draw your eye to it, and shading, which makes you believe that it actually has dimension. It jumps out at you. In mural work, you will want to save this type of contrast for those objects that are close to the viewer and seen under artificial light. For a pot that is in soft, filtered light or farther back in the picture plane, you will want to limit your shading and highlighting to the medium values.

Notice how the shading on the base of the pot differs from that on the pot itself. Because the base is made up of flat planes rather than rounded areas, each plane is shaded a uniform value. The front of the base is positioned away from the light source (upper right), so it is a deeper overall value than the top of the base, which is in the direct light. A citrus topiary from Royal Design Studio provides the finishing touch.

Establishing a Dominant Light Source

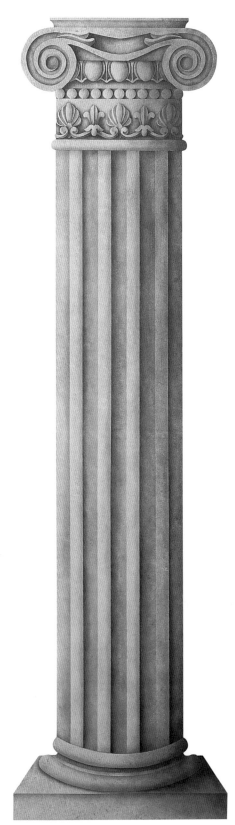

Whether you are painting and stenciling an entire mural or just a single element, you need to first establish the light source. If you look around the room that you are in, you will probably notice that there is light coming from a variety of sources and directions. There may be multiple windows or doors as well as overhead or table lighting. These varied light sources will cause ill-defined shadows and multiple shadows falling in different directions away from and on the surfaces of objects in the room.

As an artist, you will want to simplify your task of creating a convincing illusion for your viewer by choosing a single and believable light source. In the instance of a mural that contains both an interior and exterior view, there will be two light sources: the artificial light that is illuminating objects inside the room and the sunlight that is affecting objects outside, and, in many cases,

inside as well.

The choice of a light source may be very obvious. If your object or mural is in close proximity to a sunlit window, for instance, you may use that as your light source. Using a real-life source of light will only add to the realism of your illusion. If there is not a nearby or obvious source of light for your work, you will have to impose one. My standard choice is generally to have the light coming from the upper right-hand corner, which means that surfaces that are closest to that source and in the most direct line of the light will receive the most illumination. Those surfaces on the opposite side of the light source (in this case the surfaces on the lower left side) will be shielded from the light and therefore cast in shadow. Once you establish a light source, it must remain consistent.

This detail of an Ionic capital and column highlights the use of a strongly defined light source coming in from the upper left-hand side. After the shading detail was completed within the capital and column itself, the whole form was shaded darker on the right-hand side (away from the light source), to create the illusion that the entire architectural structure is cylindrical. The column and fluting detail was created entirely with tape.

Creating Carved Molding With Tape

One of my favorite techniques is creating carved molding with tape because it uses the stenciling technique to such an advantage. Even better, it is simple and doesn't even require you to cut or buy a stencil! All you need is tape, some measuring tools and a molding profile to follow, and you can create the illusion of any type of molding or trim, raised-panel effects or even carved detailing within an object. Oil-based paint cremes, which stay wet and workable for some time, are ideal for this technique because you can easily go back and reblend and smooth out any rough spots. Acrylics will be used later for the Limestone Niche and Lattice Window projects.

As with anything you are trying to copy and simulate with paint, it is very useful to have the real thing to refer to. Here are some examples of different types of molding, next to which I have measured carefully and sketched out exact profiles.

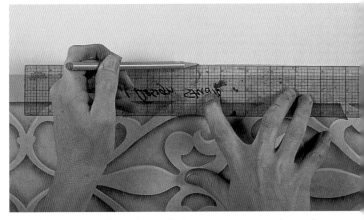

1 After copying and transferring the lines to my project with a grid ruler and light pencil marks, I start working from the bottom up. Start the shading on the bottom line and work your way up to avoid smudging the wet oil paint when you reposition the tape.

2 The length of the shadow I create depends on the depth of the area of molding I am shadowing. If it is a shallow protrusion, the shadow it casts will be small. If it is deep, the shadow will be longer. This is another device for simulating depth. Once again, I am using a medium-value gray for the shading and reserving the darker value for the deepest recessed areas. Notice how I have hugged the edge of the tape with the stencil brush, allowing only a small portion of it to deposit paint in the exposed area.

3 For the beveled area of the molding, I shade the whole area in an even value of color to represent this portion that is angled away from the light source.

4 Soft curves in the shape of the molding can be represented by running the brush freehand along an imaginary horizontal line down the area that would be curving inward. Use a very dry brush to get a more smooth, softly blended effect.

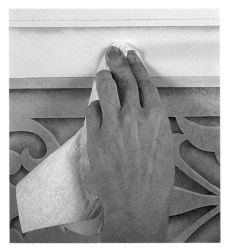

Any blotchy or uneven areas can be softened and blended by rubbing lightly with a paper towel or cotton swab.

Here is the complete crown molding atop a trompe l oeil carving created from a Florentine Grille stencil from Royal Design Studio.

por siempre jamás

Free-Form Stenciling

Free-form stenciling is using separate elements or groups of elements to create one-of-a-kind designs. While stenciled borders have a static quality and repeat at regular intervals, free-form stenciling is more artistic and natural looking—more painterly. This is most useful and effective when stenciling organic designs, such as foliage, flowers and fruit. The stenciled elements give you a quick and easy way to get the paint on the surface, with shading that creates dimension and realism. Simple details painted with a liner brush, such as veins, vines and tendrils, are added at the end to

connect the leaves, flowers, and fruit. The overall look appears hand-painted and spontaneous, artistic and one-of-a-kind.

For trompe l'oeil murals, where you are creating one-of-a-kind artwork, free-form stenciling is especially important and useful. Oftentimes, stencil artists will attempt to create free-form designs out of complicated floral border stencils. This involves isolating various elements and groupings by cutting the design apart or masking off unwanted elements with tape. This can be effective but is also very cumbersome and confusing, since the artist is trying to use the stencil for something it wasn't designed for. On the other hand, there are now many stencils designed specifically for mural

work that depict small trees, bushes, topiaries, floral arrangements, etc. These stencils work wonderfully for duplicating the exact design that the stencil artist envisioned, but they can appear static and have a limited, specific use.

Free-form stencils, however, offer many options and limitless possibilities for artistic interpretation. They allow you, the artist, the freedom to easily create something unique and site-specific. Because each item or group is individually placed, however, you must also be a designer. This can be both liberating and intimidating. There are some simple basic rules for design that you can refer to, as well as tools to help you to visualize and plan your free-form artwork.

NOTE

I first developed the concept of free-form stenciling back in 1988. I was beginning to do a lot of custom stencil work for clients in the San Diego area when I was asked to paint some bougainvillea vines on an outdoor entrance wall of a beautiful Spanish-style home. The client wanted these to be hand-painted and realistic looking as if they were a continuation of the real plants growing on either side of the doors. She definitely did not want them to look stenciled.

While I felt very comfortable and confident with my ability to paint with stencils, hand-painting realistic flowers was a skill I had definitely not mastered, and haven't to this day! So, I was off to the local nursery to find a blooming bougainvillea plant, which I brought home and studied. From it, I sketched a variety of leaf and flower shapes in realistic sizes (I measured!). I designed the flowers to be two-overlay stencils so that I could shade them and give them real depth and dimension. Some of the leaves were cut in two overlays as well, so they looked as though they were curling around themselves, for more realism.

I was then able to take these series of elements to the job, and after charcoal sketching on the wall exactly where and which way the vines would "grow," I began to lay out the design. I began with the flowers first, noticing that they grew away from the leaves. Using stencils allowed me to capture the translucent quality that bougainvillea petals have. They are very thin and papery, like onion skin. I was able to create a clean, defined edge while applying just a thin layer of paint so it looks like light is shining through them. After placing the leaves appropriately, I used a liner brush to paint delicate veins, and a round brush to paint the vine. The client was later disappointed that most people who came through the door said, "What painting?" when the homeowner asked if they had seen the painted bougainvillea as they entered. The illusion was successful!!

Here are several examples of free-form stenciling.

Hand-Painting Details

Individually stenciled elements and groupings in free-form murals need to be connected with hand-painting. For those who haven't had much experience doing freehand brush work, the idea of this may seem a little daunting. It is a skill that is fairly easy and well worth mastering, though, because it frees up a lot of possibilities for designing and contributes to the over-all hand-painted look of the finished work.

Our focus here is primarily on doing work with a script liner brush, which we will use to add veins and create connecting vines to our leaves and flowers. The script liner brush has very long bristles that will hold a lot of paint, so creating long, flowing lines is easy. Depending on how we manipulate the brush, we can get anything from very delicate thin lines to heavier vines and even branches, all with one tool. Delicate lines can also be created with a regular liner brush. For thicker branches, a small pointed no. 4 or no. 8 round brush will work well.

LEARNING TO LOVE LINER WORK

Once you become comfortable using the script liner brush, you will find it very enjoyable and relaxing to use. Like any other new skill, it just takes a certain amount of practice. Here are some additional hints to help you along.

Relax. Shake out your arm before beginning if you are tense. Painting involves your whole arm from the shoulder down, not just your wrist, so you need to be able to move freely and easily.

Practice, practice, practice. The more you do, the more comfortable you will become. Just doodle on some scrap paper. Since you will be working primarily on walls, you will need to be able to pull the brush and paint in different directions. Play with putting different amounts of pressure on the brush, and even try rotating it slightly with your thumb and forefinger as you pull the stroke to see the different effect that you get.

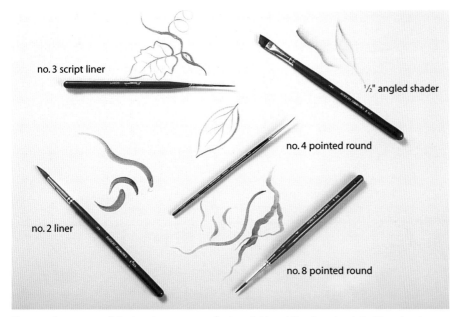

no. 3 script liner

½" angled shader

no. 4 pointed round

no. 2 liner

no. 8 pointed round

Here are just some of the brushes you may find useful in adding hand-painted touches to your stenciled murals, shown with the types of lines and strokes they can make.

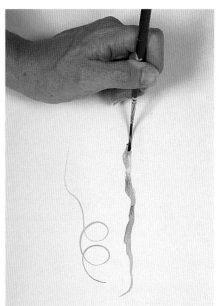

Experiment with different ways of pulling brushstrokes. For veins, begin and end each stroke up on the very tip of the brush, pulling away from the surface as you finish so the end seems to trail away. The more you press and flatten the brush, the thicker your lines will become. Using varied pressure on the brush as you pull the stroke will yield different line widths.

Make sure that you use fresh paint and thin it well. I prefer to use FolkArt Extender, but you can thin with water as well. A good ratio would be one to one. The paint should be very inky and fluid. You can adjust the ratio depending on the situation. Very transparent prints of leaves will not look good with dark stripes of veins going through them, so thin the paint more in that case. If your leaves are very dark to begin with, you might need to have more paint in your ratio, or use a darker color.

I usually use a mixture of the leaf and shading color (usually a shade of brown) for the liner work when doing the veins, and then add more of the darker color to paint the branches or vines.

Wet the brush thoroughly and rinse often in a well of clean water. Remove excess water by dragging gently across paper toweling before loading. Make sure that you load the brush well with paint. Just dabbing it once into the paint isn't going to take you very far. Load the brush by pulling it repeatedly through the thinned paint.

You should hold the brush at least midway up the handle (not down at the bottom like you would a pencil), so as not to restrict your range of motion. You may also find it helpful to rest your pinky against the painting surface to help steady your hand.

One of the nicest things about working with thinned paint is that it is erasable, as long as it's still wet. If you happen to create a less than perfect brushstroke, simply remove it immediately with a piece of dampened paper towel or sponge that you have handy (just in case).

Because the paint does stay wet awhile, you should work left to right if you are right-handed, and vice versa if you are left-handed. This way you can avoid dragging you hand through your nice fresh strokework.

I usually paint in a certain order, painting veins first, then vines, then connecting the leaves to the vines and adding last touches (such as tendrils). Tendrils must be painted very loosely, with the brush held perpendicular to the surface so that just the tip of it is touching.

Pull the brush repeatedly through the paint to load well.

Hold the brush perpendicular to the surface, allowing only the tip of the brush to make contact, for a loose, delicate line.

Liner Work Step by Step

In this demonstration, we will add the finishing touches to the group of leaves that was stenciled at the beginning of the chapter.

It is important to match the look of the liner work to the look of the stenciling. If your stenciled art is dark and heavy, your liner work needs to be darker over it to stand out. If your stenciling is soft and translucent, as in this sample, the liner paint needs to be thinned more to create a more translucent effect.

I always begin by painting the center veins first. Paint in the direction of growth, that is, from the base of the leaf to the tip. I am connecting the leaf to the stem in the process as well. Don t paint the vein out to the end of the lead; rather, pull the brush away from the surface as you near the end so that the line tapers off to nothing.

The side veins will generally conform to the outer shape of the leaf, not run in the opposite direction as shown. Erasing mistakes is as simple as wiping them away immediately with a damp paper towel or sponge!

The side veins should begin on the center vein and arc away gracefully and gently, not at right angles. Two on either side is usually sufficient. Too many veins can become busy looking and distracting.

Side-Loading Technique

Side-loading is an extremely useful brush technique. It creates the same effect as stenciling along the edge of a stencil—color is built up strongly along the edge and fades away to nothing. You can use this in your mural to visually separate elements from each other and their backgrounds where stencils and shields are not available. For demonstration purposes, side-loading is shown here for outlining a line drawing of the outer shape of a brick.

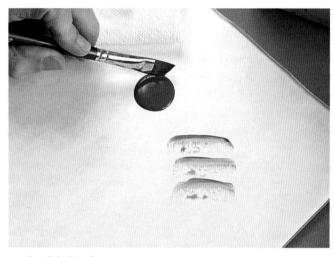

1 Load the brush
Wet the brush in a brush basin and remove excess water by laying the brush on paper towels just until the shine disappears from the brush. Dip just the corner of the short edge of the brush into fresh paint.

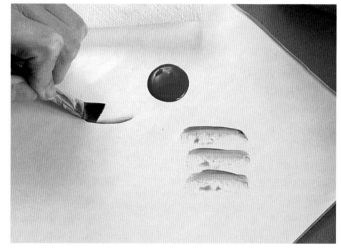

2 "Walk out" the paint
Using short strokes, walk the paint across the brush by repeatedly brushing the brush in the same direction and area on palette paper or a foam plate until you can see that the color fades from dark to light.

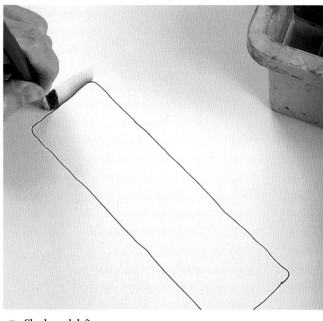

3 Shade and define
Shade around the desired area by pulling brush so the darkest value of color is right along the edge.

4 The finished effect
This brush technique takes some practice. Try drawing or stenciling a variety of shapes on scrap paper first. It is definitely a technique worth mastering!

FREE–FORM RUSTIC FLORAL WINDOW PROJECT

This step-by-step window project begins with a completed window scene and pot. It demonstrates the varied aspects of and applications for free-form floral stenciling: design layout and development, layering, shading and hand-painted embellishment.

WHAT YOU'LL NEED

- Shutter Window and Large Basketweave Pot stencil from Royal Design Studio
- Geranium and Classic Grape Ivy stencil (patterns provided on page 49)
- FolkArt acrylics: Basil Green, Berry Wine, Burnt Umber, Camel, Christmas Red, Cotton Candy, Fresh Foliage, Honeycomb, Medium Gray, Old Ivy, Olive Green, Spring Green, Strawberry Parfait, Sunflower, Wrought Iron
- FolkArt Extender
- assorted stencil brushes
- no. 3 script liner and no. 4 round
- blue tape and soft charcoal

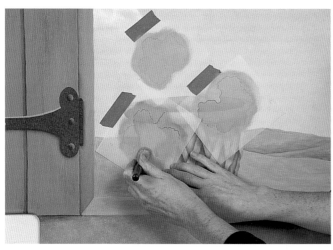

1 When working on a grouping or section of foliage, it is more efficient to lay out several elements at a time. The leaves are basecoated solidly with two to three layers of a pastel Spring Green. The predominance of white in the pastel colors makes them more opaque, providing better coverage. Use a larger 1" (3cm) stencil brush to fill in quickly. Do not add Extender to the paint at this point, as it would only add translucency when you need opacity.

2 It is important to allow each layer of paint to dry thoroughly before adding the next layer. Otherwise the subsequent layers of paint will lift the still-wet layer underneath. A hair dryer will help to speed things along.

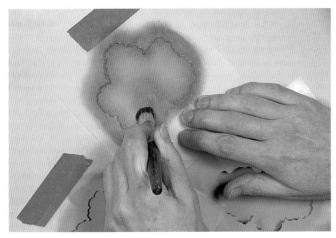

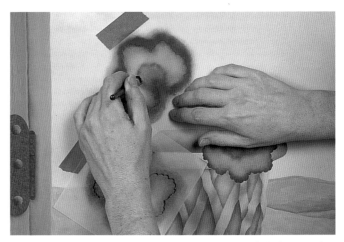

3 The leaves start to come to life with the addition of Olive Green around the edges (I'm using a ¾" [2cm] stencil brush). For geranium leaves, I also create a rounded shaded section at the base of the leaf for added dimension.

4 A blackish-green color, Wrought Iron rims the ruffled edges. For the center ring, add some Berry Wine to the Wrought Iron. Using a ¼" (6mm) brush and a tight circular motion, create a thin ring of color that encircles the center shading and follow the contours of the outer edges of the leaves.

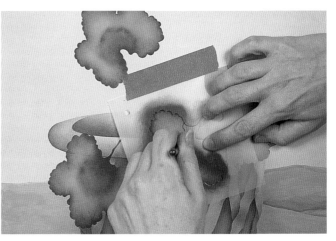

5 One of the unique properties of stenciling is the presence of an edge, a boundary to the design against which you can build up paint and color. In stenciling, we also use shields, sometimes known as friskets or fallouts, as edges. In the case of a shield, we are working with two edges. One edge covers and shields against paint, and one allows us to build up paint against it and create dimension through shading. This picture demonstrates the use of the fallout from the geranium leaf as a shield to protect the art while another leaf is stenciled just behind it.

6 After positioning the leaf fallout securely and directly over the previous stenciling, place another stencil over it, overlapping slightly so that only a portion of the new leaf will be painted. The stencil process is repeated with deeper shading using Wrought Iron. Shade where the newly stenciled leaf will appear to go behind the first leaf and appear to be overlapped by it.

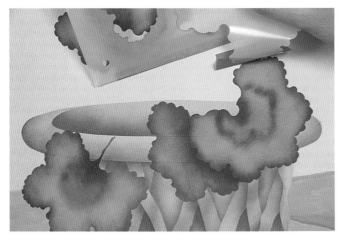

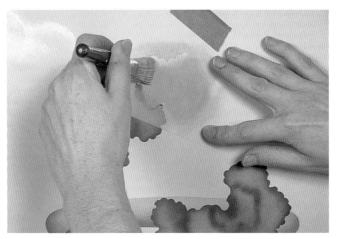

7 Notice the effect that contrast has here and the importance of proper shading. If the top leaf had been painted darker, the viewer would be confused and the illusion ineffective.

8 Many times shields are not available, or perhaps you will decide later that you want to layer something on top of some previous work. It is still possible to create shading and contrast. In this case, I am stenciling over a previously painted leaf but still want to add deeper shading where the leaves overlap for a true trompe l'oeil effect.

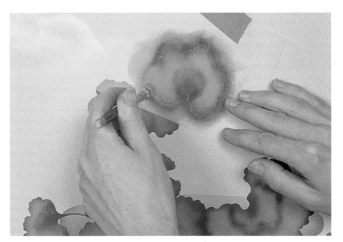

9 After completing the top leaf, replace the stencil of the first leaf and use a ⅜" (1cm) stencil brush to add darker shadow color in the area where it goes behind the forward leaf. If the fallout is available from the forward leaf, you could use that to protect it. If not, or if the forward leaf was painted too dark to begin with, you can go back and highlight it to bring it forward visually.

10 Using first the original base color, Spring Green, followed by light shading with Fresh Foliage, you can effectively bring the color back lighter. It is important to keep in mind that you can always go back and adjust colors darker and lighter as the design develops to establish the proper value and contrast relationships between the elements.

11 Once the leaves are complete, map out a nicely balanced flower placement by using small pieces of 1" (3cm) blue tape.

12 The geranium blossoms are also developed by using a layering technique, working from dark to light in value, starting with Christmas Red. The stencil has a variety of petal clusters cut into it, which can be moved around to build the flowers by creating roundish areas of petal clusters. Some of these should overlap to create more density and depth.

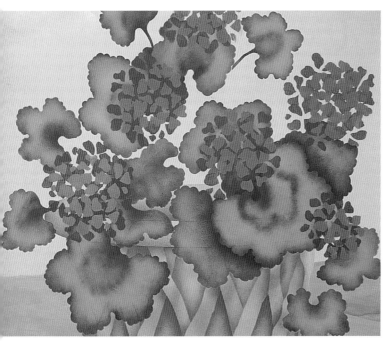

13 The second step is to repeat the process using a lighter shade of the same color, in this case Strawberry Parfait. Concentrate the second and third layers of petals in a smaller area that leans toward the light source, which is coming from the upper right.

14 After completing the third layer of flower petals with Cotton Candy, use a no. 4 pointed round brush to add short little strokes in the centers of the petal clusters. This serves to connect them and also provides more contrast and interest to the flowers.

15 The center portion of the petal clusters has a small painted dollops of both Fresh Foliage and Sunflower. Veins are added using thinned Wrought Iron and a no. 3 script liner. The veins are painted to radiate out from the center of the base, as they do in real life.

16 More contrast can be added to the flowers by hand-painting some shadows where the petals overlap each other. Use a watered-down Medium Gray and a no. 4 pointed round. It is not necessary to paint shadows for each petal. Just a few will create enough contrast to create interest, which should always be your goal!

HINT

When using thinned-down paint, mistakes are easy to fix by simply wiping with a damp cloth. Because the paint does stay wetter longer, though, you need to be careful not to drag your hand through it.

Here's the finished pot of geraniums.

17 After sketching in preliminary lines with soft charcoal to indicate the general direction the vines will grow, lay out individual ivy leaves. For a more natural, random look, place the leaves near to where the vine will be but turn the leaves in different directions for more variety. Because the leaves near the end of the vine would naturally be newer, have the leaves get progressively smaller as the vine grows out.

18 After again basecoating the leaves, this time with Basil Green, use Old Ivy and Honeycomb randomly throughout each leaf to add color and depth. Try to make each leaf a little different, using varying amounts of each color with a ¾" (2cm) or 1" (3cm) stencil brush. Allow the color to float through the leaf, and avoid creating a rounded, dimensional effect that results from concentrating color around the edges. These leaves are flat, not cylindrical.

This picture shows the same layering technique (using a fallout) that was demonstrated for the geranium. At this point, notice how each leaf has roughly the same value. There is no contrast or depth and, hence, no visual separation of the elements.

19 Here, the shield and stencil have been put back in place and deeper shading is being added by building up more depth of color.

20 This picture shows the depth and contrast, the push and pull that is necessary in trompe l'oeil painting.

21 When all stenciling is complete, add veins with a no. 3 script liner and a washy mix of the Old Ivy and Honeycomb. Where overlapping occurs, you will need to end the stroke and pick it up on the other side of the leaf.

22 Add Burnt Umber to the paint to create a darker color for the vines. The same no. 3 script liner brush is used, only this time the bristles are pressed parallel and flattened against the surface to create a thicker line. By varying the pressure on the bristles and rotating the handle between the thumb and forefinger as you pull the stroke, a varied natural-looking vine is achieved.

23 Connect leaves to the vine with the same loose stroke. You can have fun by painting the stems off in another direction before snaking them back over the vine to the base of the leaf. Be sure to attach each leaf, unless some are falling off the vine.

24 A few tendrils will add some interest and fill-in here and there. Be careful not to overtendrilize, though, or you will create a very busy and confusing-looking vine.

CREATING SHADOWS

Shadows are areas of darker tone cast by an object. The shadow will be cast onto an adjacent surface on the side opposite the light source. The way a shadow is represented on an object is determined by three things: the source of the light, the shape of the object casting the shadow and the surface on which the shadow is cast.

Sometimes it is both easy and appropriate to use the stencils themselves to create cast shadows. A good example of this would be shadows from leaves and flowers that are cast on a nearby wall that the foliage is growing over. In most cases, though, hand-painting shadows with a translucent glaze will be preferable, as well as more believable.

If the object is sitting or resting on a surface, the shadow will be connected to the object itself and projected onto the surface, and forms that are connected on the object will also be connected on the shadow. If the object is suspended, its cast shadow will be thrown and appear unconnected to it. You can represent distance from the surface by how far you distance the cast shadows from the objects creating them.

One easy way to add shadows is to stencil them using a drop-shadow technique. This involves shifting the stencil down from its original position, away from the light source. The area that is revealed is then stenciled in with a thinned, translucent medium gray, stopping short of the stenciled object with the loaded brush so as not to paint over it. Each leaf that is superimposed over a surface needs to be stenciled in the same manner. The leaves that are on the sky background would not be shadowed because there is nothing for them to throw a shadow on.

An alternative method is to use the same thinned medium gray and a no. 4 round to hand-paint the shadows following the outer contour of the shape of the object. As with the other technique, you need to represent a constant and defined light source, in this case, at the upper right again.

Use the same paint and brush to create cast shadows from the vines and tendrils.

The completed window includes a cast shadow from the pot and leaves onto the windowsill, again in the direction away from the light source.

Use these stencil patterns for geraniums and ivy. Enlarge to suit the space you want to stencil.

chapter three

CREATING YOUR OWN DESIGNS

It wasn't too long ago that precut stencil designs were limited to a few primitive-style borders or traditional Early American designs. Today there are literally thousands of precut stencil designs available that you can purchase! Computer laser cutting has allowed stencil designers to create extremely accurate and detailed multi-overlay stencils, and many stencil manufacturers specialize in designs specifically for trompe l'oeil murals (see resource section for contact information). You can find and purchase a precut stencil for all manner of flora and fauna, pots and vases to place them in, architectural elements to set them on, trellises, fences and gates to entwine them around, and even shuttered windows to view it all through!

If you can't find the right stencil element to fit your design needs, or if financial considerations are a factor (large, intricate stencils are not inexpensive), you may want to create and cut some of your own.

This elaborately designed stenciled mural by L.A. Stencilworks represents the quality and variety of designer precut stencils that are available today.

Stencil Materials

MYLAR

Mylar is a durable plastic that offers many advantages as a stencil material: It is translucent, and, therefore, you can easily see how the image you are creating relates to other images around it. The translucency also aids in placement and registration when using multiple overlays to complete a design.

The durability of Mylar means that, with care, you can use it repeatedly. It comes in a variety of thicknesses. Most precut stencils are cut from 5mm Mylar, but if you are cutting your own, 4mm will also hold up well and is a little easier to cut.

Mylar usually comes with a matte finish on one side, which is easily drawn upon. An ultrafine permanent marker is the preferable choice for transferring designs and registration marks because it will not be removed upon cleaning the stencil.

STENCIL CARD AND POSTERBOARD

Oiled stencil card is used extensively throughout Europe, and you may have seen books written by British authors that feature it. You can find stencil card in art supply stores. It is manila card that has been treated with oil to make it more durable. It is extremely easy to cut, but it has enough stiffness to allow it to hold its shape well, even when there are many elements cut out of it. The disadvantage is that it is not a translucent material, making it undesirable for detailed, multi-overlay stencils. Those same factors make it very useful, however, for cutting larger, simpler architectural elements.

You can create your own oiled card by treating manila file folder material with a mixture of one part linseed oil to one part turpentine. Mix together and apply to both sides with an inexpensive chip brush. Allow to air-dry thoroughly. The turpentine-linseed oil mixture will create a semi-translucent, durable surface that is extremely easy to cut.

POSTERBOARD

Posterboard is inexpensive and can be found in most office supply stores. It can be a good substitute for simple, larger elements if stencil card is unavailable.

FREEZER PAPER

Another method for stencil designing and cutting that works well for larger images and more graphic murals is to use large sheets of freezer paper as your stencil material. Spray the back (non-shiny) side of the freezer paper with repositionable spray adhesive, and apply the sheets to the wall in wallpaper fashion to cover the area to be stenciled. Where one sheet butts against the next, tape the resulting seam with transparent tape. Then project and/or draw the image directly on the paper and cut the separate elements of the design directly off the wall. Remove and replace sections at will while developing and shading the design.

This technique has been developed and perfected by Canadian stencil artists Linda Buckingham and Leslie Bird. A book that features this technique is listed in the resource section on page 158, and you can view some mural examples in the gallery on page 153.

E-Z CUT PLASTIC

E-Z Cut Plastic is another option for stencil cutting. It is good for blade-cut stencils but is especially preferable when using an electric stencil burner for cutting. While Mylar will tend to build up ridges or rough areas along the burned edges, E-Z Cut Plastic edges are smooth and clean. It is completely translucent and accepts and holds lines made with a permanent marker.

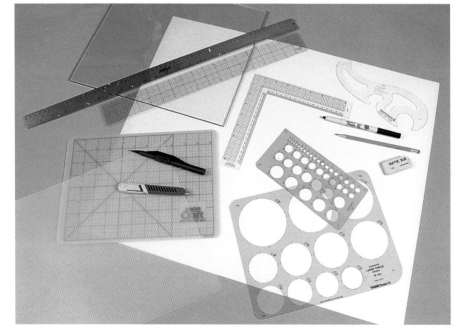

Cutting a Multi-Overlay Stencil

This step-by-step project shows you the simplest way to cut an accurate multi-overlay stencil. It begins with a clean line drawing of a classic baluster design. You can take your initial drawings or patterns to a copy center and experiment with sizes by using a copier that will reduce and enlarge. Many copy centers now have self-serve machines that allow you to increase to sizes up to several feet.

In this case, I reduced the size of the original from full-size because I wanted to create a balustrade that was set back into the middle distance of the mural, making it appear smaller to the eye. I've provided you with the pattern I'm using on page 53. Enlarge it to whatever size you require for your mural.

Knives and blades. When I began stenciling back in 1984, computer laser cutting was not yet an option. The first stencils that I purchased were actually just designs printed on Mylar that had to be cut by hand with a craft knife (actually, I used one of those large Stanley knives). I have cut many stencils since then. Long ago, I began using the smaller craft knives with the snap-off blades, and am quite used to the weight of that particular knife and the angle of the blade. Other artists prefer to use X-Acto knives, though, so you should experiment with both to find your own preference.

Cutting with a knife is especially preferable when cutting arching and straight lines. As with any new technique, with practice and experience, you will develop more confidence and accuracy.

1 Once you have determined the size of the finished design you wish to use, make several copies (it's always good to have extras). Separate the elements of the design into groups that will be included on the same overlay, and identify the overlays with a numbering system. Remember that there has to be a separation of all the elements contained on a particular overlay so that each can be painted and shaded separately. With this particular vertical design, it was easy to break it up into two overlays.

KEYS TO SUCCESSFUL STENCIL CUTTING

When cutting stencils, you will want preserve the strength of the pattern by beginning with the overlays that have the smallest elements in them. For each overlay that you cut, start with smaller elements first and work up to the larger ones to preserve the integrity of the Mylar as you go.

When cutting with a knife, you will be pulling all of your strokes toward you. Try to keep them smooth and to keep the knife moving, especially along long lines. Excessive stopping and starting will translate into jagged, ragged edges.

Try to cut each element completely before lifting the knife. When you come to a corner in the design, keep the knife tip in place as you rotate the Mylar so that you can continue to pull the knife toward you. When cutting curves and circles, pull the knife as you rotate and push the Mylar with your free hand.

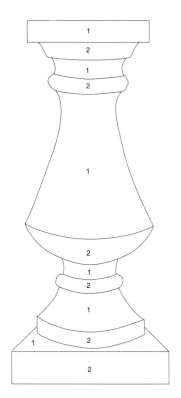

2 Experience has led me to believe that the simplest and most accurate method of cutting is to simply tape one of the copies of the design directly under the Mylar, rather than transferring the design onto the Mylar by tracing. Note: You will need at least a 1" (3cm) margin of uncut Mylar around all edges of your design. If your design is large and requires a lot of Mylar to be cut away, a margin of a few inches (10cm) will be even better, and will make your stencil more secure.

3 While some stencil artists cut stencils on a self-healing mat, my preferred method is to cut on a piece of tempered glass with rounded edges. Glass suppliers usually have scrap pieces that are available at lower prices.

Start in the middle section and work outward. Using a firm, even pressure, cut all of the #2 sections, attempting to split the drawn line as you go.

4 Use a metal ruler to aid in cutting perfectly straight lines. This ruler comes with a rubber backing on it to prevent it from slipping as you cut.

5 As an aid to registration of subsequent overlays, you should transfer other elements of the design with an ultrafine point permanent marker, in addition to labeling each overlay with a number and the name of the design. Note: With a design like this, where the elements lie side by side without overlapping, the overlays can actually be stenciled in any order. The numbering is simply for reference.

6 When finished, carefully remove the #2 overlay and place a new uncut piece of Mylar over the same pattern. Begin cutting the #1 areas. This method of cutting directly on the pattern allows you to see exactly where you have already made cuts. Notice that on this overlay I am cutting slightly inside the edge of the previous cutouts, which will create a very small overlap in the design elements, eliminating gaps.

7 When all overlays are complete, line them up to check for accuracy and to be sure that you haven't missed anything.

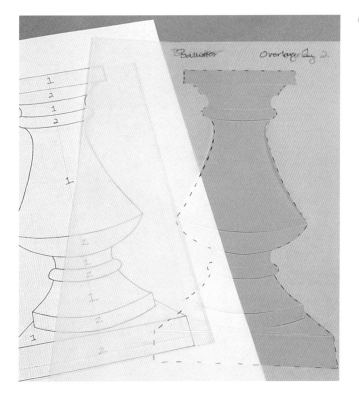

Hot-Knife Stencil Burners

A hot-knife stencil burner is an electric stencil cutter that features a pointed metal tip that actually burns through the plastic. Like a knife, the burner will take some practice and getting used to for you to be able to cut cleanly and accurately. Because you can run the tip of the burner easily in any direction (without having to move the Mylar), it is ideal for cutting things like small circles, berries, leaves and irregular edges.

Important safety tip: Stencil burners are extremely hot and can cause serious burns. Do not leave burners unattended or plugged in when not in use!

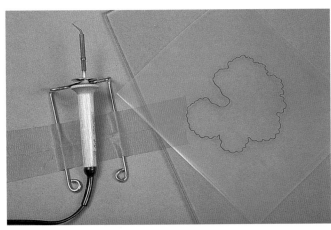

For added safety, stencil burners should be use with a sturdy stand. Tape the stand to your worktable to keep it in place.

Because you move just the tip of the stencil burner and not the Mylar, this tool is ideal for cutting small rounded areas such as these geranium petals.

The jagged, ruffled edges of the geranium leaves are another ideal candidate for a stencil burner. Just as with a knife, it takes a little practice to gain accuracy, but single-overlay elements such as these will not be ill-affected if you get off the line a little.

Quote From a Pro
STENCIL BURNING TIPS
from P.J. Tetreault, P.J.'s Decorative Stencils

Holding the stencil burner like a pencil, work in a continuous stroke, completing the entire cutout of each area (i.e., a whole leaf) before lifting up the burner tip.

Use very little pressure on the tip of the burner as you are cutting. Allow the stencil burner to do the work for you as you guide it.

For a steadier hand and smoother cut, extend the pinky finger and move it along as a balancing point, resting it lightly on the cutting surface.

Hold the stencil material tightly against the cutting surface while cutting to ensure a clean edge.

File the tip of the stencil burner with an emery board or metal nail file whenever it feels like it is dragging, or when residue builds up. This can be done carefully while the tip is hot and will help to keep it clean and sharp.

chapter four

CREATING FAUX FINISHES AND TEXTURES

The cool smoothness of polished marble. The soft nap of a velvet drape. The rough, bumpy feel of natural stone or brick. These are verbal descriptions of what your hands would feel if you touched these objects. When painting in a trompe l'oeil style, you need to provide your viewer with an accurate visual description of the object you are portraying. One way we have already learned to do this effectively is through the use of color and contrast. In this chapter, we will take that lesson one step further and concentrate on creating realistic textures with paint to represent a variety of different types of surfaces. We will also focus more on quality of shading and shading on different types of forms and surfaces. It is careful attention to these types of details that creates truly believable illusions.

Having a wide variety of interesting textures in an environment is crucial to good interior design, and designers acknowledge this aspect by combining luxurious fabrics with woven basketry, smooth polished surfaces with rough texture, etc. You will want to walk into and stay in a room that interests and delights all of your five senses, including the sense of touch. As a mural designer, you, too, can create a more interesting and inviting environment for your viewer to step into by adding the illusion of

appropriate and unique surface textures to the objects in your mural.

To create our surface textures, we will explore and employ basic faux finish techniques with paint and glaze as well as a variety of manipulative tools.

Materials and Mediums

There is a wide variety of tools available for creating textural-looking finishes and faux surfaces. Most of them are relatively inexpensive and easy to find.

WATERBASED GLAZE MEDIUMS

In order to prevent paint from drying before we have a chance to manipulate it with some sort of tool to create texture, we need to add either water or glazing medium to it.

For mural backgrounds especially, glazes and washes are an effective way to paint in skies, receding landscapes and vistas, and architectural elements incorporating stone, marble and block.

The addition of glazing medium to either latex or acrylic paint will increase its translucency and give it some body, which will allow you to manipulate it with a variety of tools and materials to create textural effects.

Waterbased glazing mediums, such as AquaGlaze, are designed to be mixed with latex paint and should be used when painting in large areas. For increased translucency and extended open time (the time that the medium stays wet enough to be manipulated) you will want a ratio of four to five parts glaze medium to one part paint. For instances where you just want to soften up the paint a bit, use a ratio of one part (or less) glaze to one part paint.

For neutral colors that are used often, premix glazing medium with latex paint and store in squeezable plastic containers. Mark each bottle with the paint chip from the color used. These containers make it easy to squeeze out just a little at a time. Foam brushes provide easy application and cleanup.

When working with glazes in large areas, use a small foam roller and a paint bucket and screen. Just dip the roller into the bucket and remove excess glaze by rolling back and forth across the screen. The excess paint/glaze will return to the bucket.

IMPORTANT NOTE

For mural work, use latex paints with a flat sheen, which will dry to the same matte finish as craft acrylics. Intermixing sheens of paint will cause dull and shiny areas in your work.

For smaller stenciled areas you can use the same craft acrylic paints and FolkArt Extender that are used for the basic stenciling technique.

When working in a smaller, limited area where you want to paint multiple layers quickly, it is oftentimes more desirable to thin paints with water to make a wash rather than use a glazing medium. The addition of water will also increase the paint's translucency and its ability to be manipulated while allowing for a fairly quick drying time. When painting these various textural techniques through the cutout portion of a stencil, extra care should be taken to work as dry as possible to avoid paint seeping under the edges, and also to be sure that the stencil is affixed securely with repositionable adhesive where necessary.

SEA SPONGE

One of the most useful tools for creating decorative finishes is the natural sea sponge. The prickly types are perfect for creating the textural look of brick or granite, but in many cases, the sponge is used primarily as a blending and softening tool, in which case it is preferable to use the backside of the sponge.

All sponges are not created equal, and each one will give a slightly different print and look, so it is nice to have a variety.

Sponges should always be used wet, but not dripping, so wring out well before using. Also, be sure to rinse and clean sponges immediately after use, as dried paint will render them unusable.

MISCELLANEOUS MATERIALS

Other readily available tools to use for creating interesting surface textures are newsprint, plastic, cheesecloth, terry rags and paper towels. Each of these materials creates a slightly different look, so raid your recycle bin and experiment!

CLOCKWISE FROM THE TOP
Larger sponges are great for blending and softening. Experiment with the looks that you get using different sides of the sponge. Large sponges can be cut or torn into smaller pieces if desired.

Sponges with a prickly surface are ideal for creating the texture of brick, granite and some types of stone.

Smaller artist's sponges work well for creating small, soft, puffy clouds and texturing in tight areas.

Sponges with a fine texture are ideal for creating large, soft clouds and highly blended effects.

BRUSHES

Besides stencil and foam brushes, it is nice to have a variety of bristle brushes on hand for creating wood finishes, dragging effects and rough, linear textures. It is not necessary to purchase any expensive brushes to produce the finishes in this book. In fact, for most finishes, cheap and well-worn brushes are ideal!

Rake brushes, as they are called, are specialty artist's brushes that can be used in small stencil areas to create fine lines for things such as fur, wood and even roughly woven fabric.

An artist s rake brush has bristles cut at different lengths, making it easy to create fine parallel lines. A dry chip brush will offer a similar effect for larger areas.

A variety of softening brushes include (from left to right) a pure China bristle brush, a Chinese hake brush (both inexpensive) and a pure badger-hair brush.

Chip brushes are inexpensive (generally under one dollar each) natural-bristle brushes and can take a lot of abuse.

Lower-quality nylon bristle brushes tend to wear out quickly, and their splayed bristles are ideal for dragging effects.

USED BRICK

The trompe l'oeil textural finishes that follow represent only a very small portion of the many types of visual effects that can be achieved by manipulating paint. I have tried to include a variety of relatively simple techniques that will prove useful for many murals beyond those shown in this book. While each mural project refers back to some of these specific techniques, you should feel free to experiment with alternate colors and finishes for any specific project. In other words, what is represented here are basic techniques that can be mixed and matched, interchanged, expanded on or simplified according to your needs.

This brick finish is easily one of my favorites! It is actually very easy to accomplish, and the addition of a few minor details, such as creating some texture in the grout and adding some flyspecking on the bricks, helps to create a more realistic illusion. It is the final addition of stenciling/shading around the edges of the bricks, however, that separates this brick technique from others I have seen.

This technique uses positive and negative stenciling. The positive stenciling is created by stenciling with highly textured natural sea sponges through the open areas of the stencil that have been cut to the size of standard brick. Upon completion of the positive areas, brick shields are used to protect those positive stenciled areas and build up shading color along the edges to create the effect of shadows created by the bricks that are protruding from the wall. The shields are the actual fallouts of the bricks that are left after the cutting process. The area that is stenciled/shaded around them is the negative area or space.

SUPPLIES NEEDED

Stencils
• Brick Wall stencil from Royal Design Studio

Pants and Glazes
• Benjamin Moore Interior Flat Latex
  Bavarian Creme (brick accent)
  Bouquet Rose (brick accent)
  Earthy Russet (brick base)
  Galveston Gray (grout accent)
  Gullwing Gray (brick accent)
  Revere Pewter (grout base)
  Soft Pumpkin (brick accent)
  Tudor Brown (brick accent)
• DecoArt Easy Blend Stencil Paint
  Ebony
  Neutral Gray
• AquaGlaze

Brushes/Miscellaneous
• two ³⁄₈" (1cm) stencil brushes
• toothbrush
• repositionable spray adhesive
• prickly sea sponges cut into small sizes (about 4" [10 cm] diameter, one for each color used)
• foam plates or paint trays
• bubble level

The finished brick presents a very convincing illusion. Notice the difference between the final effect with the shading details and the stenciled brick shown in step 8.

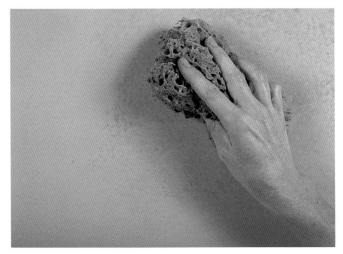

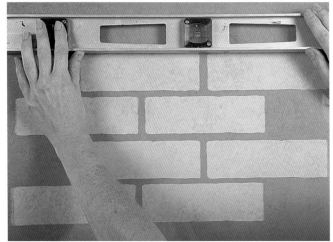

1 Basecoat area to be stenciled with Revere Pewter. When dry, use Galveston Gray (thinned 1:1 with water) to add subtle texture to the grout. Sponge the thinned darker gray on lightly with a damp sea sponge and soften immediately with another clean sponge. Hint: You don't want to create so much texture in your grout that it competes with the texture in you bricks. Keep it subtle.

2 When the background is dry, position the brick stencil that has been misted with repositionable spray adhesive to better secure it to the surface. This will help to hold the larger stencil in place and also help to keep the paint from seeping under the stencil. Check to make sure that the bricks are level. You don't want any faulty construction in your picture.

3 Put all of your paint colors on palettes or foam plates with a separate sponge for each color. I prefer to use smaller pieces of sponge (these can be torn easily), and I also choose sponges that have a lot of prickly texture to them to enhance the texture of the bricks. If you are doing a large area, add one part glazing medium to approximately four parts paint to keep the paint from drying out too quickly on your palettes and on your sponges. It is important to rinse your sponges frequently during the project since they will be ruined if paint dries on them.

4 As always, wet your sponges before use. Be sure to wring them out well so that they are just damp. Dripping water will ruin your effect and cause paint to seep under the stencil. Load the sponge with the brick base color (Earthy Russet) by dabbing into the paint, and remove excess on paper towels or newsprint.

5 Apply the brick base color Earthy Russet to almost completely fill in the stencil. Build up color by tapping up and down with a firm but light pressure to avoid pushing the paint under the stencil. In other words, don't smoosh! Make sure all of the outer edges of the bricks are well defined with paint.

6 Begin layering the brick accent colors randomly and in small, controlled areas. Try to avoid repetition of a pattern by treating each brick differently with paint colors and locations. If you have the pink color on the right side of one brick, put it somewhere else and in a different amount on the bricks around it. Don't feel it is necessary to use each color in each brick, and experiment with layering colors in different orders. As before, don't smoosh. You want to create a lot of texture, and pressing too hard with the sponge will eliminate that and will push the paint under the stencil.

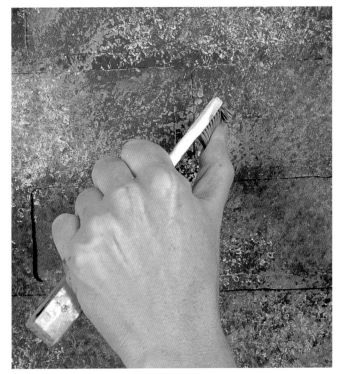

8 Here is a completed set of sponge-stenciled bricks. Continue the pattern using these same steps until the entire desired area is filled in. Always check to make sure your bricks are level with each repeat.

7 You can add a different kind of texture by flyspecking with a toothbrush dipped into the different paint colors that have been thinned 1:1 with water. Release the paint in tiny flecks by dragging your thumb across the toothbrush that is aimed towards the wall. Hint: Be sure you are wearing painting clothes, because those flecks have a way of coming back at you.

9 The precut stencil used for this demonstration comes with fallouts of the brick shapes. These are used to enhance the illusion of the depth of real brick by creating the shadows that visually separate the bricks from the grout. In this case, I have chosen to represent the light source as coming from the upper right. With a ⅜" (1cm) stencil brush, DecoArt's Easy Blend paint in Neutral Gray is used intially to create a shadow along the bottom and left side of the brick (the side opposite the light source). Additional depth and contrast is then added with Ebony along just the bottom edges of the bricks, where the deepest and darkest shading would naturally occur.

This window mural features the same brick technique used in an arched courtyard window stencil to frame a tropical scene.

STONE BLOCKS

Paper or plastic? You can create a formal block wall using ¼" (6mm) masking tape and a frottage technique. With frottage, subtle, random, stonelike patterns are created by laying paper or plastic over a wet glaze and rubbing into it.

The stone blocks can be made to any size or scale you desire, and the level of shading detail is up to you. For this example I have added quite a bit of hand-painting to create additional shadows and highlight on the blocks, as well as some cracks and pitting, but I could have

just as easily stopped after the glazing/ texture process and been left with an acceptable effect.

As with all of the techniques in this book, this one has many applications and can be used in combination with others for a wide variety of architectural applications. You can also use this effect and curved lines of tape to create stone archways and niches, or create thinner grout lines by using a smaller, ⅛" (3mm) wide tape.

SUPPLIES NEEDED

Paints and Glazes

- Benjamin Moore Interior Flat Latex
  Copley Gray (block color)
  Galveston Gray (grout accent)
  Mesa Verde Tan (block color)
  Revere Pewter (grout base)
  Valley Forge Tan (block color)
- Folk Art Acrylics
  Medium Gray
  Vanilla Cream
- AquaGlaze

Brushes

- no. 4 round
- three 2" (5cm) foam brushes

Miscellaneous

- ¼" (6mm) masking tape
- clear grid ruler
- bubble level
- putty knife
- newsprint
- 1mm plastic sheeting or grocery bags

In the finished block wall, each block has slightly different textures and coloration.

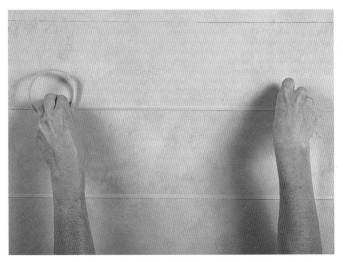

1 Over a textured grout background (previously described under the Used Brick technique) carefully measure and mark level horizontal lines for your blocks. Keep your pencil lines light, and pull the tape taught to keep it straight. The areas that are taped off will become the grout lines between the blocks when the tape is removed and all painting is complete.

2 For this example, I have made the block measurements 6" (15cm) high by 12" (30cm) wide, so after laying out my horizontal lines 6" (15cm) apart, I used a ruler to mark the tape at 6" (15cm) intervals. I then went back and ran tape vertically between two marks in a staggered pattern to create stacked blocks.

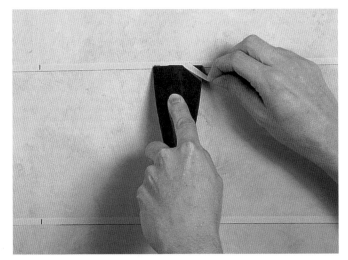

3 Leave a little tail of tape extending beyond the top and bottom of the block, which can be removed by holding a putty knife (or similar tool) firmly against the wall and pulling the tape against it. This is an easy way to tear the tape with a clean edge so that you will have clean and well-defined grout lines.

4 For the block colors, mix the latex paint with AquaGlaze at a ratio of one part paint to four parts glaze. Using one color of paint/glaze at a time, use a 2" (5cm) foam brush to paint in individual blocks, spacing the colors so that like colors are not set right against each other. Hint: Don't paint in too many blocks ahead of time before applying texturing, or you may run the risk of your glaze drying before you get to it. Paint in just a few blocks at a time.

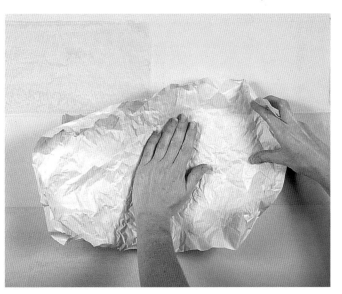

5 Crumple sheets of clean newsprint and open up flat again. You can use either packaging newsprint or the type found in pad form in arts and crafts stores.

6 Lay newsprint in wet glaze, and rub the flat part of your hand firmly across the surface. Keep your fingers together to avoid leaving your handprint in your glazed block. Alternatively, use a folded towel or rag to rub with. To add more variety of color and texture to your block, immediately rub the now-wet newsprint into an adjoining block, depositing some of the wet color onto it.

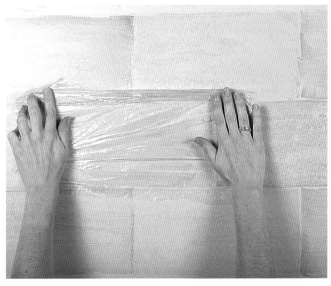

7 Mix and match blocks by using 1mm plastic sheeting cut into small pieces for a different effect. Lay the plastic in while pulling the edges taught to create horizontal lines in your print.

8 After all blocks are glazed and textured, remove tape immediately. Create further definition and dimension by painting in shadow lines on the two sides of the blocks away from the light source (upper right) with Medium Gray (thinned 1:1 with water) using a no. 4 round brush. Rather than painting a straight line, allow the brush to wiggle slightly to create the look of rough-hewn stone.

9 Paint the highlight sides in the same manner using Vanilla Cream thinned 2:1 with water.

10 Create cracks, pits and crevices by painting unthinned Medium Gray and Vanilla Cream side by side with the highlight on the bottom and the shadow on the top, using a no. 4 round brush.

REFINED LIMESTONE

There are many variations of actual limestone as well as various of ways to represent it. I developed this technique on a job where I was required to paint large columns to match an installed limestone tile floor. The technique shown here is quite simple and forgiving, fun to execute, and could be used for creating a subtle background for a wide variety of architectural elements. And by the way, it matches that tile floor exactly.

SUPPLIES NEEDED

Paints and Glazes

- Benjamin Moore Interior Flat Latex
    Stone
    Valley Forge Tan
- FolkArt acrylics
    Charcoal Gray
- AquaGlaze

Brushes/Miscellaneous

- two 3" (8cm) foam brushes
- old toothbrush
- paint trays or plastic containers
- terry towel or washcloth
- fine mist bottle (from drugstore)
- rubbing alcohol

This mural detail of an outdoor wall shows the limestone used with the carved molding technique from page 32. The Trompe L'oeil Fruit Festoon stencil from Royal Design Studio was used with detailed, controlled shading to create the look of a bas-relief carving from the limestone itself.

1 Mix one part paint to five parts AquaGlaze for each color of paint (Stone and Valley Forge Tan). Apply the mixtures simultaneously in diagonal drifts of color using a 3" foam brush. Be careful not to paint these as stripes of color. Each section should be slightly different in direction, size and shape from the others, with irregular jagged edges. Work in small areas, about 3' x 4' (9.1m x 12.2m), so that you will have time to manipulate the glaze easily and effectively. The irregular diagonal edges will blend in with the effect if you keep them light.

2 Fold a damp terry towel (wrung out well to avoid drips of water) in half and then half again. Fold back corners to create a loose but smooth pounce pad. Blend areas of color slightly by walking the pounce pad across the surface quickly in a sliding, skipping motion to break up the edges of the colors. Then pounce up and down lightly over the area. The texture of the terry towel will pull up the glaze and create little pinpricks of color that resemble the pores of the stone.

3 While the glaze is still wet, and before moving on to the next area to be painted, spritz with rubbing alcohol that has been tinted with a small amount of a Charcoal Gray. The alcohol will cause small holes and pits to open in the glaze while the mister bottle will deposit the color in small, irregular flecks.

4 Dip an old toothbrush into the gray glaze color and flyspeck by dragging your thumb across the bristles. Try not to make this too uniform. It will look more natural if some of the flecks are grouped into areas and if the specks are not all of the same size. Soften some of the flecks, especially the larger ones, by padding softly with the terry pounce. Don't press too hard or you will lift the glaze. Move on to the next area, picking up along the irregular edges of paint/glaze from the previous area.

DISTRESSED PAINTED WOOD

Don't throw away those ratty old paint-brushes! They are the perfect tool for this layered dry-brush technique that creates the look of weathered painted wood. Use this effect on trompe l'oeil fencing, paneling, outdoor furniture and tools, doors and shutters. By allowing the base color to peek through the layers, you can easily simulate the effect that time and weather have worn through a previous paint job (or two!).

For smaller areas, you may substitute an artist's rake brush or well-worn flat or round brush for the large paint brushes.

SUPPLIES NEEDED

Paints and Glazes

- Benjamin Moore Interior Flat Latex
    Decorator's White (dry brush)
    Earthy Russet (basecoat)
    Jamestown Blue (dry brush)
    Waterbury Green (dry brush)
- DecoArt Easy Blend Stencil Paint
    Neutral Gray
    Ebony
- AquaGlaze

Brushes

- two ³⁄₈" (1cm) stencil brushes
- three well-worn 2" (5cm) or 3" (8cm) nylon brushes

Miscellaneous

- Easy Mask paper tape
- light-colored watercolor pencil
- newspaper
- bubble level
- 4" (10cm) foam roller and tray

Use old paintbrushes to achieve the look of distressed painted wood.

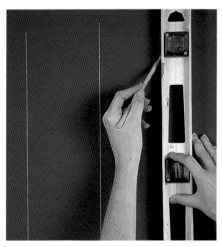

1 Using a 4"(10cm) foam roller, apply a solid basecoat of deep red or brown, which will simulate the color of the raw wood that shows though when finished. After your basecoat has dried, you can use a bubble level to lightly draw in plumb lines at intervals throughout your working area with a watercolor pencil or chalk. These will provide you with a visual reference when you are dragging your paint. Note: For photographic purposes, I have made these lines darker than I normally would.

2 Mix latex paints with AquaGlaze at a ratio of 1:1. Beginning with the blue mix, load just the tips of the bristles of a used paintbrush. Remove excess paint by dragging the brush repeatedly across newsprint so that you are working with a dry brush.

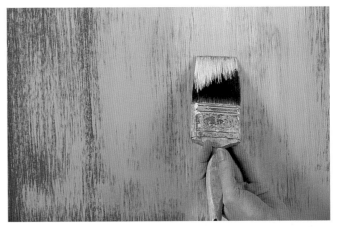

4 Repeat the process with both the green and white colors, overlapping the blue and filling in about 10 percent more of the surface area.

3 Begin applying to the surface using long, light vertical strokes. Hold the brush at an angle that is almost parallel to the surface, and use a light pressure so that just the tips of the edge of the brush are coming in contact with the surface. Begin and end each brushstroke in the air, using a "takeoff and landing" motion so that there are not any visible start and stop lines. Cover about 80 percent of the surface, leaving streaks of the background (wood) color showing through.

5 Use your bubble level and a soft pencil to remark plumb lines 6" to 8" apart (15cm to 20cm). Use two strips of Easy Mask paper tape running parallel ⅜" (1cm) apart to create an opening that will be shaded to simulate a deep groove or space in the wood. Use the Easy Blend Stencil Paint to add shading down the inner edges of the tape with a ⅜" (1cm) stencil brush: Neutral Gray along one edge and Ebony along the other.

VERDIGRIS

A verdigris finish simulates oxidation, or the effects of air and the elements on metal surfaces such as copper and bronze. There are many products on the market that actually create this chemical action, or you can use well-chosen paint colors to create the effect without the use of chemicals.

Stenciled verdigris finishes are appropriate on large planters and urns, accessory items such as lamp bases and candlesticks, and even metal fencing, grillwork and fountains.

SUPPLIES NEEDED

Stencils

- Planting Bucket stencil from Deesigns

Paints and Glazes

- Aqua Finishing Solutions Copper Dutch Metal
- FolkArt acrylics
  Basil Green
  Dark Gray
  Green Forest
  Plantation Green
  Teal Green
  Wrought Iron

Brushes

- ½" (1cm) flat angle shader brush
- 1" (3cm) and ½" (1cm) stencil brushes

Miscellaneous

- three small sea sponges
- blue tape

The completed verdigris bucket shows the stenciled finish.

1 Using a 1" (3cm) stencil brush, completely basecoat all overlays of the stencil design with Copper Dutch Metal or a similar opaque waterbased metallic paint.

2 For the darkest green color, mix a 1:1 combination of Green Forest and Plantation Green and thin slightly with water. Apply with a small, damp sponge through the main overlay of the design. Leave some areas textured and soften others by dragging the sponge across to create some vertical movement.

3 Repeat with the Teal Green, both overlapping the dark green areas and filling in previously unpainted ones.

4 Thin the final color, Basil Green, 1:1 with water and use a sponge to drag it vertically through the design, covering and softening the previously painted texture. Hint: Off-load the sponge well on paper towels before applying to design to avoid paint run-unders.

5 Replace overlays that include details of the design and repaint with the copper to separate them visually from the body of the object.

6 Repeat the process but with a lighter touch so that the elements don't just blend in with the background again.

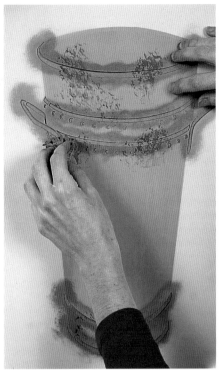

7 This picture shows the beginnings of the shading detail using a mixture of Dark Gray with a little Wrought Iron applied with a ½" (1cm) stencil brush. Note that the inside of the pot is shaded much darker along the bottom, which helps to pull the outside top of the pot forward.

8 This is an excellent example of how you can use the side-loading technique on page 40 to enhance your stenciling. This particular stencil is not cut to allow shading underneath the ridged areas, so I have used side-loading to easily create that added detail and dimension.

TERRA COTTA

Here is a great effect for creating aged terra cotta pottery, statuary, tile floors or even a distressed wall that has been ravaged by time and the environment, à la Pompeii! This technique works best when using a large silhouette stencil as the first overlay or for designs developed and defined with tape, rather than something with small multiple overlays that get pieced together. You will want to be able to create this overall texture in one shot!

For large areas, you will probably want to use latex paint and regular paintbrushes. For filling in smaller stencil designs, use craft acrylics and artist's brushes.

Great hint: You can easily create your own silhouette for many designs. Stencil out the entire design on Mylar or oiled stencil card and cut carefully around the whole perimeter, leaving yourself with one stencil (the silhouette of the design) and one fallout. Use the silhouette to lay in the entire background texture at once, follow with the individual overlays for shading and details and use the fallout for additional shading around the edges of the design where needed.

The completed design would be a great element to add height to a tropical or Mediterranean mural, or even to stand on its own as a colorful accent on a blank wall.

SUPPLIES NEEDED

Stencils
- Large Courtyard Pot and Bamboo stencils from Royal Design Studio

Paints and glazes
- Benjamin Moore Interior Flat Latex (for Courtyard Pot)
    Audubon Russet
    Delightful Golden
    Mystic Beige
    Passion Fruit
- FolkArt acrylics (for Bamboo)
    Burnt Umber   Nutmeg
    Buttercrunch   Old Ivy
    Dapple Gray   Olive Green
    Honeycomb   Spring Green
- AquaGlaze

Brushes
- three 2" (5cm) chip brushes
- assorted stencil brushes
- 2" (5cm) foam brush

Miscellaneous
- blue tape and masking tape
- oiled stencil card or posterboard
- small foam roller and tray
- repositionable spray adhesive
- ultrafine point permanent marker
- craft knife
- terry towel or washcloth

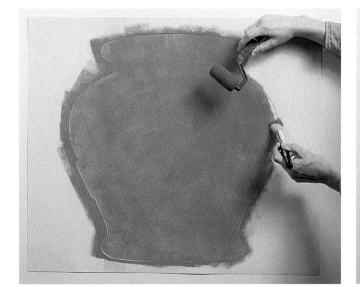

1 For this technique I first created a silhouette of a large multi-overlay pot. To create a large, stable stencil, I butted two large pieces of oiled stencil card together and ran masking tape along the seam on both front and back to secure it. I then traced the perimeter of the design onto the card through the stencil overlays with an ultrafine point permanent marker and cut it carefully with an craft knife. The silhouette stencil is secured with spray adhesive and the entire area basecoated with Audobon Russet. I like to use a foam roller for quickly painting in the interior and a stencil brush at the edges for a clean, crisp line. Allow paint to dry.

2 Use a chip brush to scrub in the peach color, Passion Fruit, in a random criss-cross fashion. Concentrate on creating a random pattern with varying thicknesses of paint, rather than a repetition of spots of color. Repeat the same technique using the yellow-toned Delightful Golden, both overlapping and filling in previously painted areas.

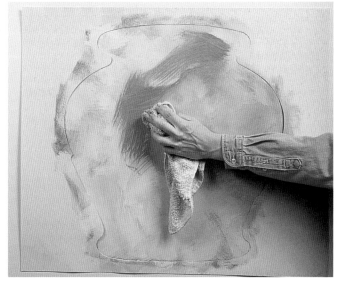

3 Immediately go back over approximately 80 percent of the entire design surface with the off-white, Mystic Beige, using the same criss-cross strokes. In some areas the underlying paint will still be wet and will blend with the top color. Some of the background colors should still show through, but they will be softened and knocked back by the off-white. Note: Be sure and carry the random colors out to the edge of the stencil design using a dry brush to prevent paint from seeping under the stencil.

4 Make a glaze using your original base color, Audobon Russet, by mixing one part paint to one part glazing medium. Apply in small areas with a foam brush, and immediately blend and rub out and around with a damp terry towel.

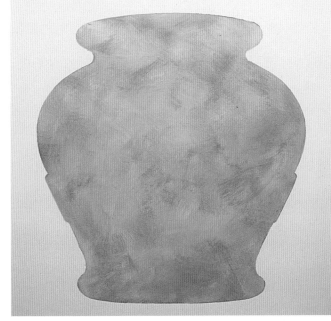

Here's the completed pot without shading.

5 Stencil and shade as usual using the design's overlays.

6 After completing the pot, I decided it would be the perfect size to hold a grouping of bamboo (see the bamboo finish on pages 87–91). Use tape to shield the top edge of the pot from the painted bamboo. Be sure to run some thin tape following the curve of the pot right along the edge to ensure a clean, smooth line.

7 In order to properly shade the inside of the pot, place tape on the bamboo stalks to act as a shield and to protect them from being painted over.

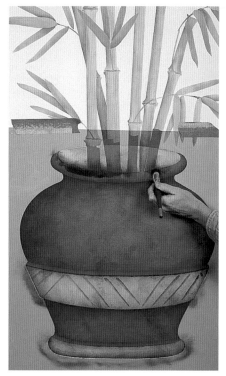

8 Replace the overlay of the pot stencil that contains the element that represents the inside of the pot, and shade it deeply along the edge and around the bamboo stalks.

9 Remove the tape from the bamboo, but keep the stencil in place to add slightly lighter shading on the stalks themselves.

10 As a final touch, dry brush in some of the Olive Green on the pot to give it more of an aged mossy look.

MARBLE

Marble finishes create a sense of cool formality, refinement and luxury. They will most commonly be used in murals in classical settings for columns, capitals, floors, panel insets, plinths and bases.

I call this finish "marbleous" because it is not meant to represent any specific type of marble, but the use of closely related, neutral colors applied in diagonal drifts and accented by the inference of veining patterns, creates an easy and effective marble finish.

Like the previous terra cotta finish, this marble finish also works best with larger silhouette-type stencils or taped-off designs.

SUPPLIES NEEDED

Stencils and Patterns
- Corinthian Capital stencil from Royal Design Studio
- pedestal pattern on page 156

Paints and Glazes
- FolkArt Acrylics
  Barnwood (marble color)
  Dark Gray (stencil color)
  Medium Gray (marble and stencil color)
  Potpourri Rose (marble color)
  Vanilla Cream (stencil color)
- FolkArt Extender
- AquaGlaze

Brushes
- three 2" (5cm) chip brushes
- no. 4 round brush
- softening brush
- assorted stencil brushes

Miscellaneous
- terry towel, cheesecloth or rag
- natural sea sponge
- blue tape
- gray watercolor pencil
- clear grid ruler and bubble level
- oiled stencil card or posterboard
- craft knife
- repositionable spray adhesive

This picture shows the completed capital, column and base. You can use this kind of creative construction to create many large but simple architectural elements for your murals.

1 Create glazes by mixing the marble colors separately with Aquaglaze at a ratio of 1:1. Apply glazes in the center of the exposed area in diagonal drifts, using either a chip brush or foam brush. Try to avoid creating a uniform striped effect; instead, lay in drifts that have a similar direction but create areas of differing shapes and volumes. Note: It is easier to create varied shapes if you lay the brush in sideways (as shown) instead of holding it perpendicular to the surface. Leave about 20 percent of the surface uncovered in the same directional, uneven shapes. These will become your negative space.

2 Use your blending tool (terry towel, cheesecloth or painter's rag) to break up the edges of the glaze, blending the colors slightly. Walk the glaze out toward the edges of the stencil with a side-to-side pushing and padding motion.

3 Hit randomly with a dampened sea sponge to blend further and create stonelike textured areas.

4 Use the pointed wooden end of the chip brush to remove the glaze and create a negative veining pattern. Vary your pressure and the angle of the brush to create a more natural appearance to the veins. Place these sparingly and allow them to follow obvious patterns that have already been created with the application of the various glaze colors.

5 With marble, especially, it is very important to soften the glazes well and often to promote the appearance that the color and texture are embedded in the surface. You will want to blend out all traces of your method of application. Any large, soft, natural bristle brush will do the trick for this technique.

6 Use an artist's no. 4 round brush and the Medium Gray glaze to add positive veins. Use a light touch and a rather jerky turning and twisting motion with the brush so that there are thinner and thicker areas, and even some spots that the brush skips. Avoid creating any straight lines.

7 Don't forget to soften!

8 This picture shows the capital after the stenciling/shading details have been completed. The column area below was originally created by measuring and taping off the desired area with a bubble level and ruler and creating the marble effect inside. Now the tape has been replaced to complete the shading, using Medium Gray.

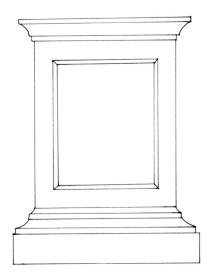

10 Cut the entire silhouette of the design. You can cut it down further into pieces to use for stenciling the edges. Most importantly, cut out the center panel for use in shading.

9 Use the stencil pattern on page 156 for the pedestal. An easy way to transfer and cut a simple pattern is to make a photocopy of it and affix it to the stencil material with spray adhesive. This eliminates the need for tracing and, in the end, is more accurate as well.

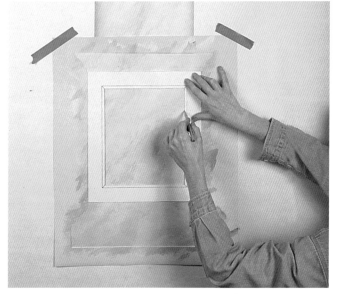

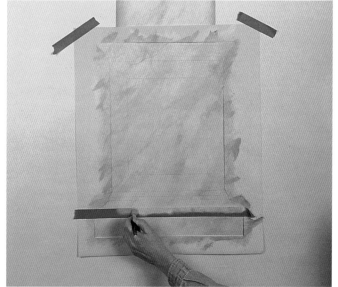

11 After base-painting the marbleous finish, transfer the lines using the stencils, ruler and a gray watercolor pencil.

12 The bottom portion of the base is shaded differently than the top. Some of these edges will be highlights painted with Vanilla Cream rather than shadows, because they will be in direct line of the light source. Rather than running the tape and shading below, highlight just above using that same stenciling/shading technique.

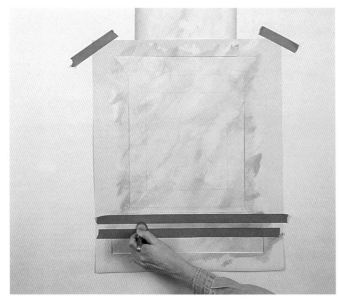

13 To differentiate the separate planes of the molding, tape off both tops and bottoms of those sections and stencil in a solid block of translucent color.

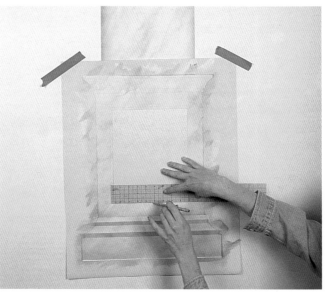

14 Measure and mark a line ¼" (6mm) out from the inner panel of the base. Here, I have simply used the spray adhesive to secure the fallout of that section.

15 Add a stenciled shadow along the top and left side edge, and a highlight on the bottom and right. Note how I have defined the corners by shielding with tape and creating more contrast.

16 Run tape or replace that cutout portion of the stencil to shade around the edges of the panel, furthering the illusion that it is recessed from the light source.

VELVET BROCADE DRAPERY

Evoke a sense of luxury and refinement by adding draped velvet around a doorway or window. Drapery treatments are easily basecoated with stencil rollers, and the painting/shading technique used with the stenciled edge makes this a simple way to create the illusion of folds of fabric.

Many stencil design companies offer elegant drapery treatments, or you can create your own by enlarging or projecting a photograph of a drapery treatment that you like from a home magazine or catalog. Most designs will involve only a two- or three-overlay stencil.

The key to this velvet technique is the use of sumptuous, rich color and even, blended, gradual shading that contours to the large, soft folds of the heavy velvet fabric. Using an allover brocade or damask pattern stencil is an easy way to add pattern and texture, and to customize the look.

SUPPLIES NEEDED

Stencils

- Large Drape stencil from The Mad Stencilist
- Small Allover Brocade stencil from Royal Design Studio

Paints and Glazes

- FolkArt acrylics
  Burnt Umber
  Huckleberry
  Licorice
  Metallic Inca Gold
  Metallic Rich Gold
  Vanilla Cream
  Yellow Ochre
- FolkArt Extender

Brushes/Miscellaneous

- assorted stencil brushes
- 4" foam roller and tray
- blue tape
- repositionable spray adhesive

Note the difference that some simple shading techniques created in the finished swag compared to the picture on page 85, lower left. After finishing the velvet drapery project, I decided it was too pretty not to be included in a mural. I then created a mural "around it" using the Dolphin Bowl and Fruit from Muracles, and the Free Form Fruit and Fleur de Lis stencils from Royal Design Studio. The blocks were created using the taping technique outlined on pages 64-67.

1 Using a 4" (10cm) foam roller, basecoat all overlays of the design with Huckleberry. Apply two coats for opaque coverage; dry thoroughly between coats. Use repositionable spray adhesive for more stability with larger stencils. I also like to go back with a large stencil brush and stencil/paint along the edges of the design to ensure a clean, crisp print.

2 After all overlays are basecoated, reposition each overlay one at a time for the stenciled pattern treatment. This can be done with a stencil brush or a roller.

3 For the stenciled brocade, mix two parts Huckleberry with one part Yellow Ochre and one part Metallic Inca Gold for a tone-on-tone effect. A little gold in the paint mix will create a little more subtle luminosity for the stenciled pattern without becoming garish or overwhelming.

This picture shows the completed brocade pattern with some of the shading and high-lighting underway. The arrow in the upper left indicates the direction of the light source.

4 This detail focuses on different depths of shading used on the opposite sides of the folds. On the left side, the fold is disappearing under another fold of fabric and is opposite the light source. This fold should receive the deepest shading with a combination of Burnt Umber and Licorice. On the right side of the fold, the fabric is rolling back under itself. Since that area will not be as shielded from the light as the other, you will still want to shade it (lighter with Burnt Umber only) to simulate a soft rounded area that is receding from view.

5 Highlights are added on the tops of the folds by using one part Huckleberry to four parts Yellow Ochre. The same tight, smooth, circular stenciling motion is used, but rather than building color along the edge, you are freehanding it, so to speak, in the body of the cutaway portion of the stencil.

6 The same technique is used with Burnt Umber to create a soft shadow next to the highlight to create contrast and some soft forward and backward movement within the folds of the fabric.

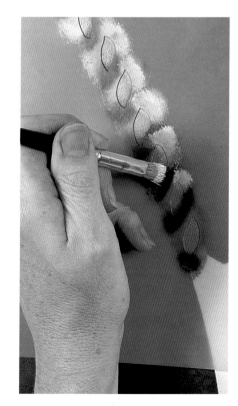

7 After a solid base-coating with Metallic Rich Gold, shadows are added on the underneath edges of the twisted cord with Licorice, with Vanilla Cream highlights painted opposite them on the top edge of the cord.

BAMBOO AND BASKETRY

Add an exotic touch to your murals with this easy technique for simulating bamboo. There are precut stencils available for a variety of styles of bamboo furniture and accessories, as well as live free-form bamboo to place in tropical mural settings. As with all of the techniques in this book, it is attention to the small, sometimes very simple, details that creates a believable texture and illusion.

Baskets are a very popular theme with stencil designers and many different shapes and sizes are available as precut stencils. One of the keys to creating interesting and successful murals is using varied textures. Many stencil artists mistakenly rely on the use of colors to represent different objects and elements within a mural. This project really demonstrates how effectively the addition of a few quick swipes with a ratty, old brush can bring an object to life.

SUPPLIES NEEDED

Stencils
• Bamboo Table and Orchid stencils from L.A. Stencilworks

Paints and Glazes
• FolkArt acrylics (bamboo table)
  Burnt Umber
  Buttercream
  Buttercrunch
  Caramel
  Coffee Bean
  Honeycomb
  Yellow Ochre
• FolkArt Extender

Brushes/Miscellaneous
• assorted stencil brushes
• rake brush
• no. 4 round (cut the bristles of an inexpensive brush at uneven lengths with scissors)
• 2" (5cm) chip brush
• blue tape
• palette or foam plate

Here's an overall view of both the bamboo table and basket of orchids.

A NOTE ON COLORS
Although they are not specifically part of this project, these are the colors I used to make the orchid and basket.

• FolkArt acrylics (orchid): Ballet Pink, Burnt Umber, Lemonade, Olive Green, Raspberry Sherbet, Rose Pink, Spring Green, Wrought Iron
• FolkArt acrylics (basket): Brown Sugar, Burnt Umber, Licorice, Teddy Bear Brown, Warm White

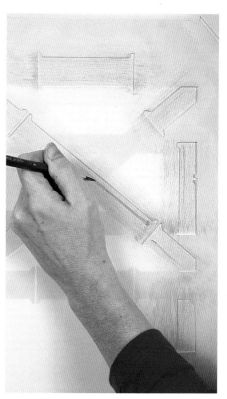

1 Basecoat entire table design solidly with Buttercrunch. While this demonstration focuses on one overlay only, each overlay will be replaced, one at a time, and the texture detail added before any shading begins.

2 Put some Yellow Ochre out on a palette or foam tray. Dip chip brush in water and pull some paint out, dragging across the tray and through the brush to load it slightly with the thinned color. Drag the brush lightly through all of the cane openings, following the long direction of the canes. A light touch will keep the paint from going under the stencil and will produce thin scratchy, irregular lines.

3 Use Honeycomb (thinned 2:1 with water) and a no. 4 round brush to create some long slashed lines in some of the canes. These indicate the areas where the bamboo fronds were stripped from the canes after harvesting.

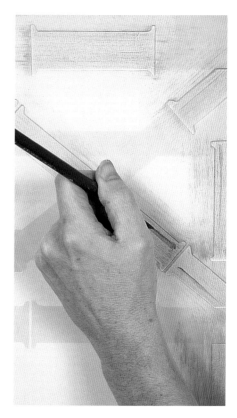

4 Use Caramel and a no. 4 round brush to create a thin shadow line on the edges of the slashed lines away from the light source.

5 Using the no. 4 round brush again, apply highlights on the opposite sides with Buttercream.

6 Because this stencil design leaves unpainted gaps between the canes, I have painted this in with Honeycomb and a no. 4 round brush to add to the overall handpainted look.

7 Additional texture can be added over the lines created with the chip brush by using a smaller rake brush and thinned Honeycomb (2:1 with water) to create more depth and interest.

8 This picture shows the texturing completed on each overlay. Because the shading and highlighting that follows is done with thinned, transparent paint, the texture will show through. You will always want to complete your texturing steps completely before shading. The texture is on the surface and will be affected by light and shadow in the same way as the object as a whole.

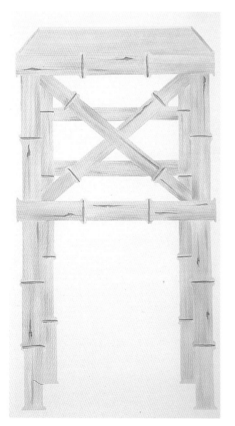

9 The shading is completed with Caramel to create the rounded effect of the canes, and a mixture of Coffee Bean and Burnt Umber to create the contrast shadows that separate the elements and add depth to the painting. Use a ¾" (2cm) stencil brush for all shading.

10 This detail emphasizes the importance of properly applied shading where there are so many overlapping elements. Each element that is overlapped by something in the foreground must be shaded darker at the overlapping point to place it behind visually.

11 In this second detail, notice how I have used the freehand stencil shading to create a soft shadow under the areas where the canes bump out at their ends.

This project is near completion. I have left the basket portion of the design for this demonstration with only the basecoat of Brown Sugar completed and ready for its texture treatment.

12 Use your uneven no. 4 round brush to add some texture detail here and there along the woven wicker, following the direction of the weave, of course.

13 Repeat.

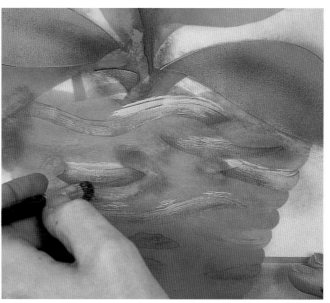

14 For more control over where the texture is applied, replace the stencil overlays. This will allow you to texture the top and bottom edges of the wicker without the chance of applying paint in the wrong places.

15 Once the texturing is complete, apply shading details. As usual, you will want to shade darker on the sides of the elements that are blocked from the light source and where overlapping occurs.

HEAVY METAL

Ironwork is used extensively in Mediterranean and Mexican types of architecture and design and you will find stencils available for iron sconces, shelves, fencing, grillwork and decorative items such as this candlestick.

This technique creates a heavy, dramatic look and is best suited to use with bold, dramatic colors in murals such as deep warm golds, reds and rusts.

SUPPLIES NEEDED

Stencils

• Italian Candlestick stencil from L.A. Stencilworks

Paints

• FolkArt Acrylics
Gray Mist
Licorice
Light Gray
Maple Syrup
Persimmon
Wrought Iron

Brushes/Miscellaneous

• assorted stencil brushes

• four small natural sponges

• blue tape

Stencils are available for decorative ironwork, such as this completed candlestick.

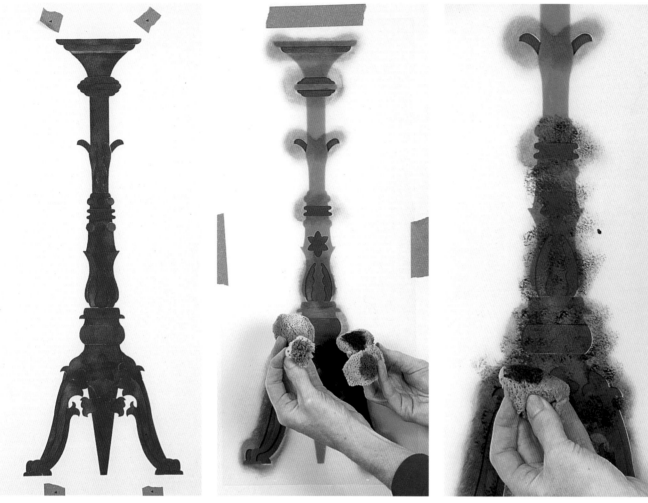

1 With a 1" (3cm) stencil brush, apply a solid basecoat to the entire design with Wrought Iron.

2 For fine texturing on metal, use smaller natural sponges to apply the following unthinned paint colors randomly. These sponges have a more delicate texture than the larger sea sponges, with fine holes throughout and are easier to control and manipulate. Use one for each color.

3 Beginning with the darkest color, Licorice, apply random texture throughout the design, leaving a lot of open space. Be sure to off-load excess paint from the sponge onto paper toweling before applying to your stencil!

4 Now apply the Light Gray in the same manner. Try to vary the amounts of all of the colors in the separate portions of the design so as not to create the look of a pattern.

5 Continue with the Maple Syrup. Notice that each sponge creates a slightly different type of print. Don't forget to keep changing the direction of your hand to avoid repetition of prints.

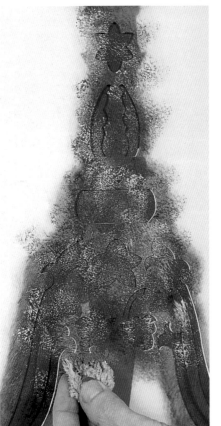

6 Apply the Persimmon last, selectively. This is a very strong color, and you will want to keep it to a minimum.

7 Once the texturing is complete on all overlays, replace the stencils and define the form with a careful studied use of highlights and shadows. Use a ⅜" (1cm) stencil brush to stencil Licorice for the shadows and Gray Mist for the highlights. Add extender to the shading colors for easier blending.

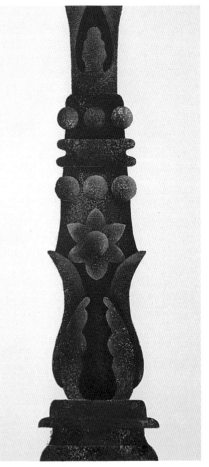

8 This detail shows how creating a highlighted contrast effectively catches the eye and pulls those areas toward the viewer. Keep your highlights and shadows just along the edges of small cutout areas of the stencil.

FAUX BOIS

The centuries-old art of reproducing various types of fine woods with paint is known as *faux bois*, which is French for "fake wood." Traditionally executed using multiple layers of rich oil glazes and expensive tools and softening brushes, it is truly an art form in the hands of master artisans.

For the purposes of providing the look of wood graining in a quick and easy fashion, I have included a technique I like to call *faux faux bois*, or *faux bois light*. You can use this technique for painting wooden beams, doors and furniture in your murals.

SUPPLIES NEEDED

Paints and Glazes

- FolkArt acrylics
   Yellow Ochre (basecoat)
- FolkArt Pure Pigment Colors (glazing)
   Asphaltum
   Raw Sienna
   Raw Umber
- AquaCreme

Brushes

- two 3" (8cm) chip brushes
- 2" (5cm) chip brush
- 3" (8cm) foam roller
- no. 10 round
- softening brush

This faux bois section was completed in only a matter of minutes and is a very believable representation of wood graining.

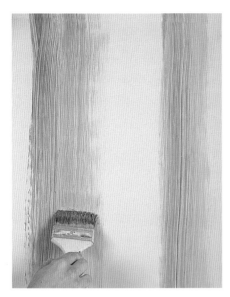

1 Basecoat the entire area to be painted with a solid application of Yellow Ochre using a 3" (8cm) foam roller. Mix two separate glaze colors. The lighter color will be a 1:1 mix of Asphaltum and Raw Umber and the other will be Raw Sienna. To one part pigment, add three parts AquaCreme glazing medium. Using a 3" (8cm) chip brush, apply the lighter glaze color to the surface first using long, vertical strokes, creating a random stripe effect.

2 Using another chipbrush, fill in and overlap the unpainted areas with the darker glaze, blending and softening the edges where the two colors meet by continually dragging the brush through them. It is preferable to have some unevenness of color depth, as visible in the top portion of the picture.

3 After the surface has been coated and blended, begin adding some detail and interest to the woodgrain in the form of knots. Use a clean 2" (5cm) chip brush to pull through the glaze. Begin by pull-ing a thinner line by holding the brush so that just the edge of the brush is being dragged vertically through the glaze.

4 Using a continuous motion, turn the brush as you are pulling so that the bristles flatten out more on the surface as you pull the brush around an imaginary knot in the wood.

5 Revert to the original position of the brush as you complete the stroke. Repeat the same procedure as a mirror image (identical, but reversed) on the other side of the knot.

6 To further establish the knot, bring the brush back down the middle, executing a U-turn around the knot.

7 A more detailed option is to then pull the brush through the glaze using a skipping, side-to-side motion, which will create subtly wavy lines in the grain. Soften everything lightly with a softening brush.

8 Use a no. 10 round brush and the darker glaze mixture to create more contrast and definition around the knots and here and there throughout the grain. Soften.

chapter five

COMPOSITION, COLOR AND PERSPECTIVE

We have already focused on creating depth and dimension in single stenciled forms and objects in chapter two, and studied the creation of textural illusions in depth in chapter four.

Much of the remainder of this book shows various stenciled mural projects to further illustrate a variety of techniques and applications that can be used as building blocks for creating trompe l'oeil stenciled murals. Each one is an important lesson unto itself, and although each one is presented with a different and singular project, it is the appropriate application of any or all of these techniques and principles to each mural that you paint that will result in a higher level of artistic success.

Besides presenting a variety of easy step-by-step murals you can re-create for yourself, my goal with this book is to provide you with the inspiration, confidence and techniques to create unique, one-of-a-kind pieces of mural art of your own design, from your own imagination, for your own specific purposes. In order to do that successfully, you need to be aware of some general rules for good design and composition. While planning your composition and executing your mural, there some basic principles of organization that you should keep in mind: balance, harmony and variety, movement, dominance and, of course, contrast.

There is space in this book only for a brief overview of these important principles. For more in-depth study I highly recommend taking drawing and design classes through a local resource such as adult education, community college or studio classes. There are also some listings in the resource section on page 158 that you may find valuable.

This Stone Cottage mural illustrates how various aspects discussed in this chapter work together to create a pleasing composition. Every aspect is deliberate, even the placement of the daisy on the shelf, since it leads the eye back down to the flower bed along the bottom of the picture.

Composition

As a mural designer and painter you have no real limitations on the variety of subject matter and the type of composition that you choose to paint, other than that of size and scale, which will be determined by your site. You may be creating a composition for an entire room, a single wall or a small shelf. Once your working area is determined, you may choose your subjects and arrange and manipulate them at will.

The key to success is in organizing your composition and subject matter to the best advantage. You will want to create a pleasing, harmonious and believable arrangement and illusion that will interest your viewers, draw them in and lead their eyes through your mural.

SYMMETRICAL BALANCE

The simplest way to achieve balance in a composition is through symmetry. If you imagine a vertical line running through the middle of your mural with identical objects (or sizes of objects) equally distributed on either side, you will have achieved symmetry, and balance along with it.

ASYMMETRICAL BALANCE

Asymmetrical balance involves creating a felt equilibrium between all parts of the composition. Balance can be achieved not only by an even distribution of the weight and size of objects but also by balancing such things as a small area of strong color with a large area of empty space. Because there are no set rules to dictate asymmetrical balance, the artist must feel, judge and estimate the ways that the various elements and their arrangements will balance each other in the total composition.

HARMONY AND VARIETY

You can create harmony in a composition by introducing repetition and rhythm. Repetition and rhythm are inseparable because rhythm is actually the end result of repetition. Repetition of forms is an easy way to unify a mural. Some classic examples of this in mural work are the repetition of architectural elements, such as columns and balustrades, and the repetition of landscape elements, such as similar types of trees and flowers, or even repetition of shapes and colors.

Variety is the counterweight of harmony and provides the other side of organization that is essential to unity. While repetition of forms helps to bind the picture together as a whole, variety adds essential interest to the total work. For instance, a balustrade or the repetition of fence posts creates rhythm and unity in a mural. It is the introduction of an element with a contrasting line, shape or color against that pattern that grabs and holds the attention of the viewer.

MOVEMENT

Movement in a composition is what visually binds the various elements of a mural together and helps to draw the viewer's eye through the picture. You can achieve this by directing lines and shapes toward each other in a way that keeps the viewer's eyes moving in a self-renewing way. In other words, you want to keep bringing the focus back into the mural, not out of it. Foliage and trailing vines are an easy and obvious tool for this. Rather than creating a vine that shoots off and out of the picture frame and takes your viewer along with it, you can plan the direction of growth so that it visually leads one's eyes to another element in the mural.

DOMINANCE

In mural work, a sense of dominance is generally created by making an object or group of objects into a focal point. This is usually the foreground object that the viewer's eye is initially drawn to and represents the most important element in the mural. If each object is given similar or equal importance in the composition, the lack of contrast that is created will provide a confusing image that gives no direction to the viewer.

CONTRAST

Our eyes are naturally drawn to contrast, and contrast should be used as an aid to creating dominant focal points. Contrast comes in many forms in the composition of a mural: Contrasts of sizes, shapes, values, colors, textures and directions of lines are all key to creating interesting and exciting visual images.

Symmetry   Limestone Niche

This is a good example of symmetry, even though there is some difference between the left and right side of the bromeliad (just
enough to add interest). Symmetry makes for a very pleasing and
balanced arrangement that is easy to design and excecute.

Asymmetry   Lattice Window

This is an asymmetrical arrangement set against a unifying backdrop
element, the lattice. The strength of the orchid in the basket is well-
balanced by the more delicate bougainvillea, primarily because of
the intensity of their color. The ferns along the bottom, like the lattice,
provide a unifying element.

Movement   Romantic Window

The dynamics and movement created by the direction of the trailing foilage in this mural ensures the viewer s eye will keep moving throughout the composition in a circular, self-renewing way.

Dominance   By-the-Sea

Even though there is not a lot to look at in this composition, the shells sitting on the ledge are made to be the most important element because of their dominance in the mural. The fact that they are placed in the foreground in a still-life arrangement and are painted with the greatest amount of value contrast makes them the first thing to catch the eye.

Contra s t   Round Brick Window

The contrast that is created by the dark bars against the distant landscape and the red bricks brings your eye directly to the foreground of the picture, which is exactly where the artist wants it to be. Likewise, the contrast of the purple/blue flowers on the red brick holds our attention there as you follow the graceful curves of the twining vine with your eyes.

Color Basics

USING COLOR

Color is the one element of composition and painting to which we are most sensitive, the one that touches our emotions and arouses our senses. A pleasing use of color is essential. You may be trying to create a serene, elegant mood through the use of cool neutrals, or an exciting and dynamic composition full of vibrant color. Whatever the case, some basic understanding of the general principles of color theory will prove helpful.

HUE

Hue is the property or characteristic of a color that refers to its position on the color wheel. It refers to the color name, such as yellow or green.

VALUE (OR TONE)

Value refers to the lightness or darkness of colors, or the quantity of light that a color reflects. To change the value of a color, you must mix it with another pigment that is darker or lighter in character. Note: The only pigments that will change the value of a color without altering the hue are black and white.

INTENSITY

While value refers to the quantity of light that a color reflects, intensity refers to the quality of light in a color. The intensity of a color, or hue, can be bright and saturated or dull, grayed and neutralized.

TEMPERATURE

Color temperatures fall into one of two groups: warm colors and cool colors. Red, orange and yellow, the colors of fire and the sun, are considered warm colors, while blue, green and violet, the colors of the sky and water, are cool. The temperature of a specific color can be made warmer with the addition of a warm color or cooler with the addition of a cool color.

Quote From a Pro
from Susie Wolfe, CDA
Color Theory Expert and Educator

Adding a small amount of the same color to all of the colors in your palette is called adding a "mother color." This will harmonize all the colors in your mural. This "mother color" could be gray, an earthtone or any neutral color.

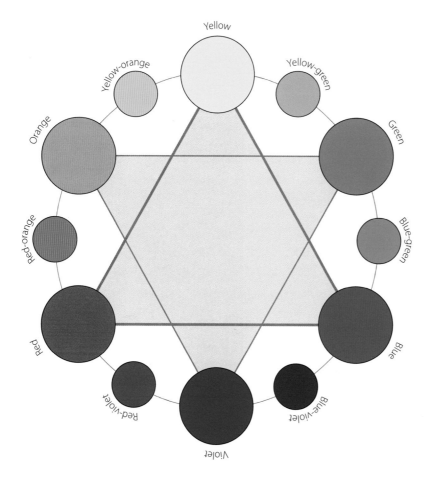

Creating More Depth in Your Murals

SIZE

Size is simple to depict. The farther away an object in the mural is from the viewer (i.e. the closer to the horizon line), the smaller it appears. To effectively represent great depth and distance in a stenciled mural, it is important to include objects of different scales and to have them positioned correctly in the picture plane according to their sizes.

COLOR

As a general rule, objects in the distance are duller and those that are closer to the viewer appear more vivid in color and intensity. This is due to atmospheric conditions. When painting areas and objects that are near the horizon line, and therefore more distant, use more toned-down or grayed colors. As you move forward in the composition, objects should be more colorful, so choose brighter, warmer greens for shrubbery, more vivid colors for flowers, and brighter blues for water in the foreground.

CLARITY

The same atmospheric conditions that affect color also affect clarity. Objects in your mural that are placed in the foreground, close to the viewer, should be painted in greater detail and more intense colors. Objects that are placed farther away, in the middle and background, will be less distinct. Their colors will be closer in value and painted with less contrast.

CONTRAST

Areas of lower contrast will recede into space. High contrast between values creates crisp, well-defined edges that appear to come forward in space. Painting areas in your murals with a variety of different values is a sure way to add depth to your work. Closely related values naturally recede, so they should be used for distant objects and landscapes. Also note that painting with closely related values makes edges, even stenciled edges, appear softer. Using a heavy contrast in values attracts the eye and brings an object or area to the front, so use the most intense contrast in values in the foreground of your painting.

TEMPERATURE

In general, cool colors seem to recede while warm colors seem to advance. In the case of trees and shrubbery, for instance, using duller and cooler shades of green for the background foliage will help to keep it in the distance. Adding more warmth to your foliage, that is, adding yellow to the green, will help bring greenery forward.

A NOTE ON DEPTH

Imagine the difference between a sharp focus in the foreground and soft, blurry focus in the background. As images become more distant from us, we notice less intensity of color, less value contrast, softer edges and the smaller scale.

Perspective

The dictionary defines perspective as "a technique of depicting volumes and spatial relationships on a flat surface," and also "the manner in which objects appear to the eye in respect to their relative positions and distance." A detailed study of perspective and its wide range of mechanical rules would be impossible and impractical in this book. We will limit our investigation and use to simple one-point linear perspective, two-point perspective and aerial perspective. For more in-depth study, there are several good books listed in the resource section.

LINEAR PERSPECTIVE

Linear perspective involves a system for representing depth by means of converging lines at a point, or points, on the horizon. It is a system of representation that was developed at the time of the European Renaissance as an aid toward representing the appearance of reality.

AERIAL PERSPECTIVE

Aerial perspective relies on the fact that as objects recede into the distance, there is a reduction in color intensity and clarity. Consequently, you can use both color and clarity as tools to easily create a sense of depth in your stenciled murals, to push objects back and to help reduce the flat look that is all too common.

TWO-POINT PERSPECTIVE

Two-point perspective is used for creating open windows, gates and doors. While there are a variety of precut stencils available that feature these elements, they may not fit your particular design needs and measurements. With some simple measuring and planning and the use of tape as your edge, you can easily create an open window or door to represent any angle or point of view.

POINT OF VIEW

While stencils are very useful for easily painting and shading elements, they do have one drawback for use in mural work: They are designed and cut to represent only one view, one perspective. It is not a matter of simply redrawing a line, as in freehand painting, so you must be careful to correctly position the stenciled object in the mural according to the point of view that it represents.

A good example is a stencil of a clay pot. If a clay pot is placed below our eye level, we will be able to see inside it, and to see that it is, in essence, a cylinder. It will be represented to us as rounded on the top and bottom. The closer we are to the pot, the more we will be able to see the inside surface. If the clay pot is placed at our eye level, the roundness at the top and bottom will be represented as straight horizontal lines, and we will

see only the outer surface of the pot. If it is placed at a point above our eye level, the top edge will be represented as a curved surface, only the curve will arch up. We will not be able to view any of the interior surface of the pot. In fact, if it were not resting on something, we would actually be able to see the bottom of it.

SCALE

As objects recede from our view they appear to become smaller. Therefore objects that are placed near the horizon line (the greatest distance from the viewer) need to be proportionally scaled down from the objects that are placed in the foreground. To help understand this concept better, it is helpful to look at a perspective floor grid. Richard Tober of A Matter of Perception has created a step-by-step model on the opposite page. You can follow the steps to create a grid for any mural project to assist you in determining the scale and placement of design elements in your mural, and/or you can use this grid technique to plot out tile and floor designs for your murals.

The perspective floor grid is also the beginning step for creating perspectively correct open doors, windows and gates and will be used later in the By-the-Sea mural.

HOW TO CREATE A PERSPECTIVE FLOOR GRID

1. Select a horizon line, usually located at eye level. We selected 40" from the floor.
2. Select a vanishing point on the horizon line (the point at which all parallel lines converge). Attach a string to the VP.
3. Measure and mark the floor tile widths at the bottom of the grid; these tiles should be equal.
4. Stretch the string from the VP to the tile points, mark dashes with a watercolor pencil and use a straightedge to draw in the converging lines.
5. The floor grid consists of square units. Select a tile depth that is about half of the tile width; this creates a three-dimensional effect.
6. Using a straightedge, intersect the first floor tile on the diagonal and mark where the straightedge intersects with each parallel line. This tells you how small the tiles become as they recede into the background.
7. Use a level to draw in each of the tile depth lines.

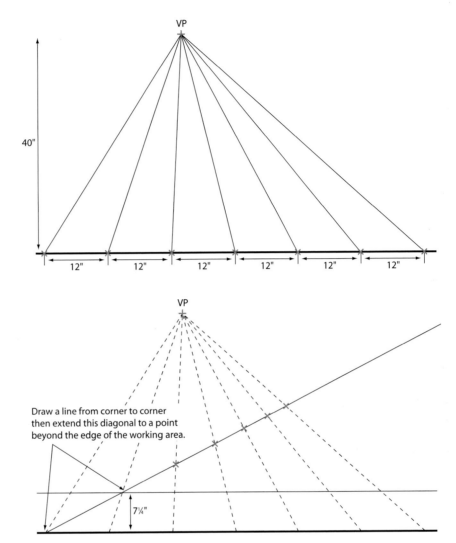

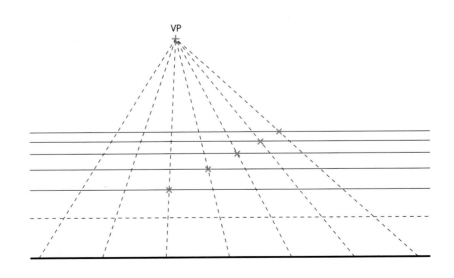

Draw a line from corner to corner then extend this diagonal to a point beyond the edge of the working area.

SKYSCAPE

Any mural that incorporates an outdoor scene will also naturally include a sky, and there are many variations on techniques for creating interesting skies with paint and glazes. Sunrise, sunset and moody or stormy skies can be very dramatic and colorful and create quite a focal point. In landscape painting, for instance, oftentimes the sky is the most important element in the picture and can be painted with great detail.

In most stenciled murals, however, the sky is merely a part of the background, a backdrop for the more detailed elements that make up the mural. In most instances, you will want to keep your sky fairly simple and unassuming, but a very interesting and believable effect can be achieved simply by fading color with softened glazes, and using small sponges to create layers of soft clouds.

As always, it is easier to paint something believable if you have a visual reference to go by, so gather a collection of pictures of skies that you can use as a starting point. Differing atmospheric conditions produce a wide variety of possible cloud formations. The skyscapes in this book feature what I consider to be classic clouds. They are the soft, puffy, cumulus variety that come to most people's minds when they think of idyllic summer days, and so they create a very recognizable and acceptable backdrop.

All of the skies that are featured in the murals in this book are painted with the same easy and effective technique.

SUPPLIES NEEDED

Paints and Glazes
- Benjamin Moore Flat Interior Latex
  Harbor Fog
- FolkArt acrylics
  Barnwood
  Ultramarine Blue
  Wicker White
  (optional colors: Bayberry, Potpourri Rose
  and Purple Lilac)
- AquaGlaze

Brushes/Miscellaneous
- higher-quality 3" (8cm) nylon paintbrush
- softening brush
- small natural artist's sea wool sponge
- large natural sea sponge
- spray bottle (optional)

This completed skyscape shows the finished clouds. Note the variety of depth and shape and also that the clouds become smaller and less distinct as they near the horizon line, simulating a greater distance from the viewer on Earth.

1 Basecoat the sky area with a solid, even coat of Harbor Fog. For this technique, you will need to work fairly quickly in the next step. The idea is to get a uniform, blended effect while pulling soft cloud shapes out of the wet glaze with a dampened sea sponge. For small, limited areas, such as in window murals, this should not be a problem. If you are working on a large mural with a large expanse of sky, you may want to ensure some more working time by wetting the wall with a 1:1 mixture of water and glazing medium. This can be applied easily with a spray bottle. Because you are now working wet-on-wet, you will have more time to manipulate, blend and soften the glaze over a large surface.

Note: Because of the additional layer of glaze, it will take longer for your sky area to dry and cure. Wait until it is completely dry before attempting any additional painting work over the area.

2 Blend Ultramarine Blue with Harbor Fog to deepen the color. Mix a washy latex glaze with one part Harbor Fog–Ultramarine Blue blend to four parts glazing medium. To that mixture, add 10 percent water. Beginning at the top of the surface, apply the wash with a foam roller or higher-quality paintbrush using long horizontal strokes.

3 In nature, the color of the sky will appear to lighten and become less intense as it nears the horizon line. This is caused by the fact that we are viewing it through the layer of heavier, hazy atmosphere that is closest to the Earth. To replicate that effect, feather your glaze out more thinly with the brush as it nears the horizon line. You may even go back to the top, while it's still wet, and add an additional layer of blue to deepen it there.

4 Working quickly while the glaze is still very wet, use a dampened sea sponge to push out soft cloud shapes. Basically, you are opening up the darker blue glaze back to the lighter blue background. The soft contrast between the colors creates the diffused, subtle look of the background clouds. Pushing more forcefully with the sponge here and there will create a variety of depth in the cloud colors even at this early stage in the process.
Note: The bottom edges of the clouds should appear to run horizontally, parallel to the surface of the Earth. The billowing occurs on the top edges of the clouds, extending into the atmosphere.

5 As you work over the surface with the sponge, immediately soften the edges of the clouds by brushing very lightly with a softening brush. You are really just tickling the surface with this brush so that you are just softening the top layer of the glaze, not moving it around. Vary the direction of your brushstrokes. Also soften the areas that have been just brushed in with glaze to remove the lines left by the brush. In this case, if the brush lines are running horizontally, soften by brushing vertically. I call this softening against the grain.

6 Once your background of negative clouds is dry, you can begin creating more distinct layers of positive clouds. Negative refers to the fact that you are creating an effect or shape by removing the paint/glaze. Positive refers to the fact that you are applying paint to create a shape. Use a smaller artist's sponge to apply white acrylic paint. To create a less harsh effect, I first press my sponge into some glaze medium before loading it with the acrylic. Notice that I am holding the sponge so that it rounds up at the top. Just the top portion of the rounded area has been loaded with paint so that the effect is one of a distinct print at the top of the cloud that fades into the blue at the bottom.

7 Work back to front, layering your clouds forward as you go. If your more distinct positive clouds are layered over the softer negative ones, a realistic sense of depth is achieved. You do need to be constantly aware, though, of designing your cloud shapes. They should appear flatter, with a more horizontal line on the bottom. You want a lot of variety. Do not allow your clouds to be of all the same shape and size, or to be spaced evenly apart. It is also important to not end all of your clouds at the edge of your picture frame. Create a sense that life is going on outside of your window by showing just small portions of much larger clouds at some of your edges.

8 Optionally, you can add some subtle color into your clouds by sponging in washes of thinned colors, such as Bayberry (green), Potpourri Rose (mauve) and Purple Lilac. Keep these very light and soft. Create even more dimension and realism by lightly sponging the bottoms of your clouds with a very soft warm gray, such as Barnwood. Be sure to soften any additional colors or washes that you place in your clouds with either a damp sponge or softening brush.

ROUND BRICK WINDOW

A trip to the lumber aisle in the local hardware store was the inspiration for this mural in the round. I was looking for alternative surfaces for the murals in this book, things that were readily available and easily movable. My idea was to provide mural options other than those painted directly on the wall surface, so that murals could move with their owners to different houses and apartments or from room to room. After spying these perfect circles precut from pressed particleboard, I set to work trying to figure out a suitable design for them.

A round brick opening seemed an easy and obvious choice. The bars were brought in to add another texture and element to the mural, and to provide a structural support for the morning glory vine. The addition of the decorative detail in the middle keeps it from looking like a jail window! I had a lot of fun painting it and ended up being very pleased with the uniqueness of the final result.

You could substitute stone blocks or marble for the brick for a more Mediterranean or formal look. Or, for a nautically themed room, you could use the cut round board to create a port hole!

SUPPLIES NEEDED

Stencils and Patterns

- Morning Glories, Victorian Grille and Foliage stencils from Royal Design Studio

Paints and Glazes

- Benjamin Moore Flat Interior Latex Harbor Fog

- white waterbased primer (suitable for wood)

- FolkArt acrylics
  Aspen Green (background, trees)
  Basil Green (foreground, trees)
  Bayberry (foreground, trees)
  Bluegrass (background)
  Buttercup (trees)
  Cinnamon (grille)
  Clover (morning glories)
  Coffee Bean (trees)
  Dark Brown (grille)
  Dark Gray (bricks)
  French Vanilla (bricks)
  Dove Gray (grille)
  Gray Plum (distant trees)
  Lavender Sachet (morning glories)
  Licorice (grille)
  Light Periwinkle (morning glories)
  Limelight (morning glories)
  Mushroom (trees)
  Plum Chiffon (morning glories)
  Raw Umber (bricks)
  Spring Green (landscape foreground)
  Wrought Iron (grille)

- FolkArt Extender

Brushes

- assorted stencil brushes

- no. 8 filbert and no. 8 round

- 1" (3cm) flat

- no. 3 script liner

- 2" (5cm) foam brush

Miscellaneous

- blue tape and ¼" (6mm) masking tape

- repositionable spray adhesive

- 4" (10cm) foam roller and tray

- small natural sea sponge

- Mylar, acetate or posterboard

- 36" (91cm) diameter circle cut from ¾" (2cm) pressed hardboard

- clear grid ruler, string, pushpins and pencil

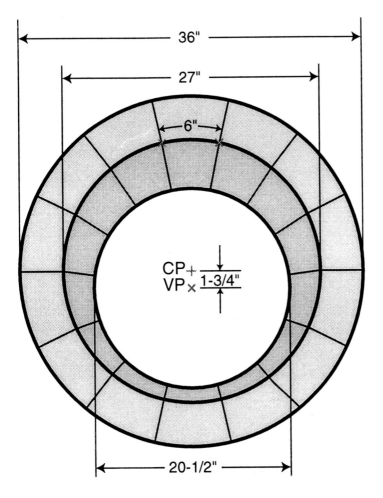

1 Basecoat front and sides of board with two to three coats of white waterbased primer. Use a 4" (10cm) foam roller for the smoothest effect. Tie a length of string around a pencil, pull it taught along a ruler or yardstick and make a mark on the string with a permanent marker at 11½" (29.2cm) and 13½" (34.3cm). Use a pushpin at the 11½" mark on the string to secure the string at the eye level mark near the center of the circle (see "VP" on pattern). Holding the pencil perpendicular to the surface, trace a complete circle. Reposition the string so that the pin intersects the 13½" mark and place the pin in the center point. Trace another line. The outer circle indicates the face of the brick, which is flush with and on the same plane as the inside wall.

2 Now that you have a reference as to where the scene will be placed in the circle, using a 2" (5cm) foam brush, base in the center area of the circle and a little beyond with Harbor Fog and paint a skyscape down to the horizon line according to the instructions on pages 106–109.

With a 1" (3cm) flat artist's brush, basecoat the foreground with a wash of Bayberry thinned with water. With a no. 8 filbert, paint a stand of distant trees using Gray Plum. Applying paint with a jerky, scrubbing motion will create diffused color and soft edges.

3 Repeat the same painting technique using Basil Green to create a closer group of trees. Use a small natural sponge and Aspen Green to create some subtle treetops with a varied texture.

4 Create more depth in your landscape by painting in additional washes of color. Use cooler, grayer greens such as Bayberry and Bluegrass in your background, and warmer, yellow-greens such as Spring Green in the foreground. Because cool colors seem to recede and warm colors advance, this will aid in your illusion of depth.

5 Beginning with the darker Aspen Green, stencil the various shapes that will become the more distinct foliage of trees seen in the near distance. Overlap the darker areas of foliage with the lighter Bayberry and Basil Green. Using a variety of different shapes placed randomly and at different heights will ensure that each tree appears unique and natural.

6 Sketch in the basic lines of a tree in the foreground with soft charcoal. Use a different foliage pattern with the same stenciling technique to create layered groupings of leaves that extend primarily from the ends of the branches.

7 Use a no. 8 round to paint in the trunks of the trees using Mushroom. Notice that the color has been thinned to more of a wash for the distant trees, so that the lack of contrast allows them to fade more into the haze of the background. The foreground trunk is painted in a sharper focus with a deeper concentration of color and the addition of Coffee Bean for contrast.

8 More contrast, warmth and light can be brought into the foreground tree with the addition of a yellow color, Buttercup, to the top layer of foliage.

9 When the landscape is complete, shield it by cutting a circle from Mylar or posterboard to the diameter of the inner circle, 21" (53cm). Use your pencil, string and pushpin again to create a perfect circle, and secure in place with spray adhesive. This will remain in place until the entire brick texturing and shading has been completed. Basecoat the entire brick area with a light gray and sponge with a darker gray wash according to the brick instructions on pages 60–63.

10 Use your string again, from the center point, to redraw the outer circle.

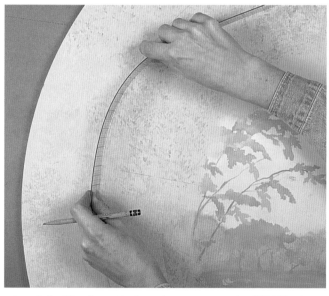

11 A flexible, clear grid ruler makes it easy to mark off 6" (15cm) increments along the circle.

12 Use a ruler to draw grout lines on the outer face of the brick that extend from the edge of the brick directly to the center point of the circle. Draw lines from the outer edge of the inside face of the brick to the eye level point, which is lower than the center point of the circle.

13 Use ¼" (6mm) tape to mask off the grout lines, either bending it around or cutting it and changing directions at the corner where the face of the brick changes direction. The inner circle represents the portion of the brick or block that extends through the wall space to the outside. Be-cause of our point of view, we can see most of it, although we can see more of the top inside area because our eye level (on the horizon line) is dropped below the center. If eye level had been placed dead center, we would see an equal portion of the inside of the brick all the way around. The grout lines of the outer face of the bricks would seem to extend in straight lines through the inside face to the center point. The slight change in direction of the grout lines, which occurs by the slight adjustment of the eye level, adds a great deal to the illusion.

14 After completing the brick painting and shading techniques outlined on pages 60–63, remove the protective shield to complete the painting. Because the primary light source is coming from the outdoors and the upper left, paint a definite highlight in the inside face of the bricks using a highly thinned wash of French Vanilla.

15 Paint a translucent shadow on the remaining area of the inner face of the bricks using a mixture of Raw Umber and Dark Gray.

16 Create more contrast between the highlight and the outer face of the bricks by defining that edge with some of the shading color. Allow it to fade out to nothing from a sharp edge.

17 Use a bubble level and pencil to make plumb lines that will become the iron bars. The bars themselves are ⅜" (1cm) thick and are spaced 3¼" (8.26cm) apart, beginning in the middle of the circle. Use 1" (3cm) tape to define the straight edges, and ¼" (6mm) tape to create a curved end. The bars should be placed in the approximate center of the inside face of the bricks.

18 Basecoat the iron bars with Wrought Iron. Create additional texture according to the steps outlined in the Heavy Metal technique on pages 92–94, using a small sponge to apply random patches of Dark Brown and Cinnamon. With a ⅜" (1cm) stencil brush, shade the bars on the side opposite the light source (right) with Licorice. Highlight on the side closest to the light source (left) with Dove Gray.

19 To add some decorative detailing to the iron bars, I adapted a section of the Victorian Grille from Royal Design Studio. I created the design by using only a portion of the original and flipping it to create a mirror image. Alterations of stencils are best worked out on paper first. You can stencil out a proof, make multiple copies and cut and paste until you find an arrangement of elements that works best for your purpose. Refer to your paper proof as you stencil to easily determine which elements you want to paint and those you need to tape or shield off.

20 Sketch in a free-form vine arrangement, in this case Morning Glories from Royal Design Studio. Use a ¾" (2cm) stencil brush to basecoat the leaves with Limelight and the flowers with Lavender Sachet. Create some dimension and interest in the leaves by shading darker with Clover.

21 Notice here that the green of the leaves has been highlighted and set off from the green background with the addition of Lavender Sachet, the flower color. The flowers themselves are shaded with Plum Chiffon.

22 Use a combination of Limelight with a painted shadow of Clover to add definition to the delicate veins and vines that connect the morning glory vine using a no. 3 script liner. Define and shade the morning glory flowers with Light Periwinkle and Plum Chiffon using a ⅜" (1cm) stencil brush.

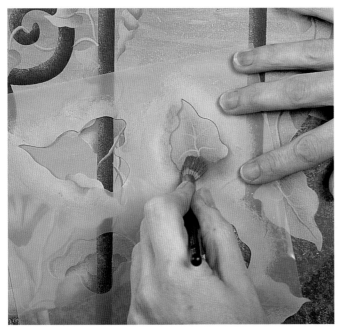

23 It is always desirable, and creates a more interesting and unified composition, if you allow your colors to travel through and reflect off each other. In this case, use the deep floral color, Plum Chiffon, in a selective way to add more realism and depth to the leaves. The addition of Clover to certain areas of the flowers will have the same positive effect on them.

24 The final touch is to handpaint cast shadows using your thinned shadow glaze of Dark Gray. As always, these shadows mimic the shapes of the objects that are casting them, and will fall in the direction that is opposite the light source.

LATTICE WINDOW

A lattice background provides a great backdrop filler that unifies the mural area while providing a means of support for a multitude of twining and vining plant options. These can grow in from the outside, providing a visual connection between the interior and exterior of the mural. The shallow shelf/ledge can be used to display a pretty plant, such as this tropical orchid and basket, providing even more color and interest to the mural.

WORKING WITH TRELLISES AND LATTICEWORK

You can use trellises and latticework to create simple but formal support structures and architectural elements that visually connect different areas of your mural. A trellis with some sort of colorful vine and flowers growing through it is a great vertical element that takes your viewer's eye up and through your mural.

Latticework, fencing and trellises can be easily executed by using tape and careful measuring, or using the large variety of precut stencils that are now available. They can be created by using either a positive method or a negative method, meaning that you will either be taping off or using a stencil to define the lattice background (positive), or taping off and shielding the lattice itself (negative).

POSITIVE LATTICEWORK

In the case of positive lattice, you will be painting your structure, usually in white or off-white, after the entire background has been completed. You can follow the measurements of real lattice and framing to plot out and tape off a multitude of lattice configurations. Tip: Getting the white paint to cover the previously painted background may require two to three coats of paint. It is always important when painting multiple coats to allow each layer of paint to dry thoroughly before repainting. If the previous layer is still slightly wet, you will run the risk of lifting the paint in those areas. Use a good-quality acrylic paint that has good coverage. White latex paint has less pigment and will take more coats, with a longer drying time between coats.

NEGATIVE LATTICEWORK

The term negative implies that we are painting the space around the actual element. That means if your latticework is white, you will need to start with a white background.

Our project involves an arched lattice opening with a negative stencil, through which we see a sky background, so the painting will be done in blue, leaving the unpainted areas to become the effect of the white lattice. The working surface is actually a shape that has been cut from ¾" (2cm) MDF (medium density fiberboard) with a router and hung like a large picture or mirror. The advantages of this are that you can move your mural around at will after it's finished, and the real dimension of the wood adds to the illusion of depth. You could paint directly on your wall surface, of course, or paint the design on PolyMural Canvas (see resource section), cut it out and mount it with wallpaper paste. If the wall surface is properly sized, you will be able to remove your mural at a later date and hang it elsewhere.

SUPPLIES NEEDED

Stencils and Patterns

- Classic Garden Lattice, Bougainvillea and Sword Ferns stencils from Royal Design Studio
- Orchid stencil from L.A. Stencilworks
- full-size blueprint of pattern available from Royal Design Studio

Paints and Glazes

- Benjamin Moore Flat Interior Latex Harbor Fog
- FolkArt acrylics (for sky and lattice)
  Barnwood
  Medium Gray
  Ultramarine Blue
- white waterbased primer (suitable for wood)
- AquaGlaze
- FolkArt Extender

Brushes

- assorted stencil brushes
- no. 3 script liner
- no. 8 round

Miscellaneous

- clear grid ruler and soft charcoal
- 1" (3cm), 1½" (4cm) and ¼" (6mm) blue tape
- large natural sea sponge
- terry towel or washcloth
- ¾" (2cm) medium density fiberboard cut to shape

A NOTE ON COLORS

Although they are not specifically part of this step by step project, these are the FolkArt acrylic colors I used for the orchid, basket, bougainvillea and sword ferns.

- Orchid and basket: Ballet Pink, Brown Sugar, Burnt Umber, Lemonade, Licorice, Raspberry Sherbet, Olive, Rose Pink, Spring Green, Teddy Bear Brown, Warm White, Wrought Iron
- Bougainvillea: Clover, Dusty Peach, Olive Green, Red Orange
- Sword ferns: Clover, Dapple Gray, Italian Sage, Thicket

1 Basecoat the MDF in a waterbased white primer. Use 1½" (4cm) tape to define the bottom and side edges of the window. This will create a frame for the lattice.

2 To accurately mark in a 1½" (3.8cm) thick arc for the top of the window, use a clear grid ruler to make little tick marks about 2" (5cm) apart and 1½" (3.8cm) from the edge. (My edge was made round by the router, so I am measuring in from the top point of the curve.)

3 Stretch ¼" (6mm) tape (which curves easily because of its thinness) to connect the tick marks in a graceful arc. Add wider tape on the outer edge to further protect the surface from unwanted paint.

4 Position the lattice stencil so that it is centered in the arc and so that you will end with some crossed lattice at the point where it crosses the frame. Begin stenciling using a 1" (3cm) brush with blue glaze (Harbor Fog deepened with Ultramarine Blue crylic, mixed 1:1 with latex glazing medium). Be sure to off-load the brush well. See the Skyscape project on page 106 for specific instructions.

5 To add some subtle depth and variation, you may want to immediately pull out some soft cloud shapes with a dampened sea sponge. Continue stenciling the lattice in all directions from the starting point, right into the edges of the taped frame.

6 Use a combination of Barnwood and Medium Gray to create a soft shadow line on the lattice with the stencil (use a ½" [1cm] or ¾" [2cm] stencil brush). This particular stencil includes an overlay for the short dashed shadow line running in one direction, and a long continuous line (like a stripe), running in the opposite direction. The "stripe" is created by moving the stencil overlay along as you go. In order not to have a hard-edged stopping and starting point, allow your color to fade out to nothing before reaching the end.

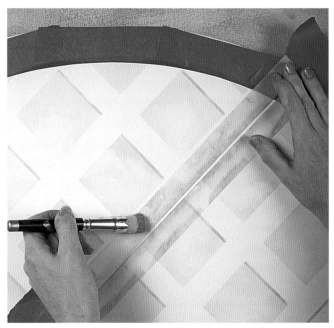

7 Move the stencil forward and pick up the stenciling where you allowed it to previously fade out to nothing. These shaded lines, or planes, indicate the narrow side edges of the lattice.

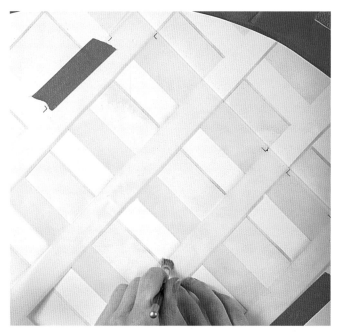

8 Use the first overlay with the cut squares positioned strategically where the lattice strips appear to cross, to shade right up into the edge with the stencil brush and Barnwood, creating a cast shadow on the underneath lattice strips.

9 Shade similarly on the lattice strips where they meet up with the outer frame. Note: Don't shade the blue areas of the sky. The shadows will only occur on actual surfaces, not in the atmosphere!

10 Here is a detail of the completely shaded lattice and window ledge. The molding underneath the ledge was shaded according to the instructions outlined in chapter two for creating carved molding with tape. Weave your way through your mural. One of the really fun and easy things to do with free-form floral stencils is to manipulate them in and out and around architectural elements in a mural. It also adds more to the overall sense of depth and realism in your work as well.

11 I have used two different types of free-form stencils for this project, Sword Ferns and Bougainvillea. Where I want my foliage to go behind the lattice I can simply protect it with pieces of tape or replace the stencil. With the stencil in place, I can use various shades of green to create layers of ferns growing outside the window.

12 To allow the ferns to come inside, remove the protective stencil or tape and paint over the lattice. In this case I am using another piece of Mylar taped in place to shield the bottom edge of the fern where it goes behind the lattice.

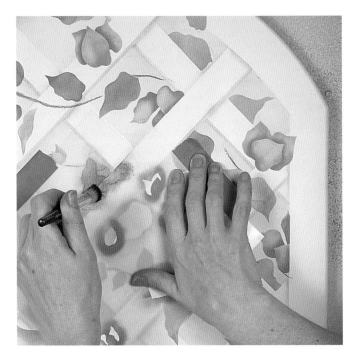

13 The free-form Bougainvillea is painted and woven through the lattice in the same manner. The charcoal lines were sketched in first to establish the direction and form of the vines.

Where the floral design of bougainvillea grows in front of the lattice, I have simply painted as usual. Where I want it to go behind, I have shielded the lattice portion with tape. The tape protects the areas of the lattice I want to avoid painting over, and also provides an edge against which I can build up shading contrast.

The orchid in a basket stencil from L.A. Stencilworks was the perfect element to complete the composition. See the page 119 for specific colors used.

14 Cast shadows are added with the same Barnwood–Medium Gray mix that was used to shade the lattice. Thin the color with additional extender or water to make it more translucent. Mimic the shapes of the elements onto the lattice only (not the sky).

15 When I was finished I decided that the white lattice was too clean and boring looking. I simply took the thinned shading paint and dragged it across the lattice with a terry towel, in the direction of the grain of the wood. Sometimes these subtle little extra details can make all the difference!

LIMESTONE NICHE

Creating a classical, curved niche is an effective way to create an interesting architectural feature on an otherwise blank and boring wall space. A niche is an excellent way to extend the illusion of space in tight quarters, such as a hallway or small bathroom. The fairly deep shelf offers a multitude of options for bringing in additional color and/or interest. I have chosen to include an elegant and classical pot and simple plant, but you may choose a colorful vase of flowers, a stack of books or an urn of abundant fruit, to name a few options.

This mural project is suitable for beginners because you are only concerned with portraying shallow depth and can focus on developing the strong contrasts of values that are inherent in architectural trompe l'oeil. This particular project was painted on ¾" (2cm) MDF (medium

density fiberboard) that was cut from a paper pattern with a router. The dimension and thickness of the material helps to aid in the illusion, and also creates a movable mural that can be hung where you wish. You may notice that this is the exact same shape and pattern that was used to create the previous Lattice Window Mural. A few changes in tape placement and shading patterns, and voilà, you have a completely different mural!

An additional lesson to be learned from this project is how to create the illusion of an architectural carving from a simple theorem-style stencil design. You can use this technique to create a bas-relief-style carved ornament from any multi-overlay stencil that features classical lines and large, connected design elements.

SUPPLIES NEEDED

Stencils and Patterns

- Large Shell Onlay, Large Acanthus Leaf Pot and Bromeliad stencils from Royal Design Studio
- blueprint of niche dimensions available from Royal Design Studio

Paints and Glazes

- FolkArt acrylics
  Barnwood (shell onlay and niche)
  Barnyard Red (bromeliad)
  Charcoal Gray (shell onlay and niche)
  Country Twill (pot)
  Dapple Gray (bromeliad)
  Dark Gray (pot)
  French Vanilla (shell onlay and niche)
  Glazed Carrots (pot and bromeliad)
  Italian Sage (bromeliad)
  Licorice (pot)
  Medium Gray (shell onlay and niche)
  Metallic Antique Copper (pot)
  Olive Green (bromeliad)
  Wrought Iron (bromeliad)

- FolkArt Extender
- AquaGlaze

Brushes

- no. 4 and no. 8 round brushes
- assorted stencil brushes

Miscellaneous

- blue tape
- repositionable spray adhesive
- Mylar or E-Z Cut Plastic
- craft knife
- tracing paper
- clear grid ruler
- hair dryer
- small artist's sponge
- ¾" medium density fiberboard cut to shape

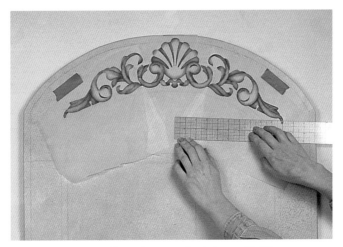

1 After creating an allover limestone finish (pages 68–69) on your working area, transfer the working lines of the pattern using a ruler and pencil. These will be defined later with tape and stenciling/shading, as well as some simple hand-painting.

Here, on tracing paper, I have stenciled a proof of the stencil design I intend to use to create my bas-relief carving, which helps to determine a pleasing and properly centered placement of the element.

2 Stencil all overlays of the design using a sharp contrast of values to define each element using a ⅜" (1cm) stencil brush. Because the desired effect is to have the stencil design appear as if it is carved from the same limestone as the niche, concentrate the stenciling just around the edges of the design elements while allowing the background finish to remain intact and visible. Each shape is defined with Barnwood, and a mixture of Medium and Charcoal Gray are used in the most deeply recessed areas of the design, which would naturally receive the least amount of light.

3 In order to visually lift the design from the background and complete the illusion, a shield needs to be created and cut. Stencil the complete design accurately onto Mylar or E-Z Cut Plastic or paper. With a craft knife, cut carefully around the whole perimeter of the design to create a shield against which you can shade and define the outer edge of the stencil design.

4 After spraying lightly with repositionable spray adhesive for a secure hold, affix the shield carefully in place so that is lines up accurately with the design. Use a ⅜" (1cm) stencil brush and Medium Gray paint to shade around the entire perimeter of the design. Use the darker Charcoal Gray to then shade a deeper value and a sharper contrast on all of the underneath edges of the design, which would be opposite the light source (above).

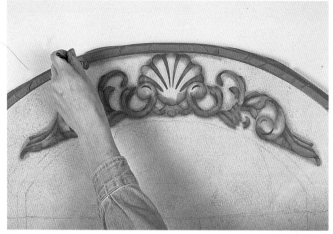

5 Thin French Vanilla slightly with either water or extender. Use an artist's brush to hand-paint highlights on the top edges of the design. Pick out those edges that would most naturally be in direct line with the light source, which is coming from above.

6 Because the shell onlay is positioned on top of the molding detail, replace the shield before proceeding to your stenciling/shading with tape. Use flexible ¼" (6mm) tape to define the curve and burnish well. Add 1" (3cm) tape on the outer edge to protect the surface you don't want to paint. Stencil/shade a dark shadow below the edge with Charcoal Gray.

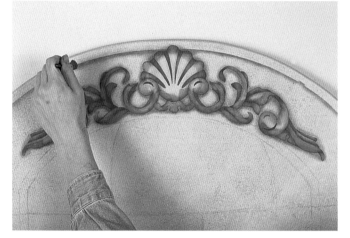

7 After removing the tape, soften that edge and create some roundness to the opposite side by stenciling/shading along the line. Use the lighter Medium Gray color and a firm, even pressure with a very dry brush.

8 Continue the same process for both sides (inside and outside) of the outer carving that runs across the top and down each side of the niche.

9 Position tape so that it defines the inner niche, using both the ¼" (6mm) and 1" (3cm) tape again to define the top arch. Use a large stencil brush loaded with Medium Gray and a sweeping motion to bring the shading down into the curve. Define the edges further with Charcoal Gray.

10 The molding under the ledge is shaded in the same way as the previous Lattice Window. To define the edge of the ledge, use tape and a light pressure to create just a subtle contrast where the plane of the top edge of the shelf meets the plane of the front edge. Both would naturally receive a lot of light, but with it coming from above, the top edge of the shelf would be slightly more illuminated. As always, you need to create contrast between different elements to visually define them, even if it's just a little!

11 Use your tape to define the curved back edge of the shelf and shade the wall behind with Medium Gray, then the deeper Charcoal Gray.

12 Remove the tape and add some depth and color with Medium Gray.

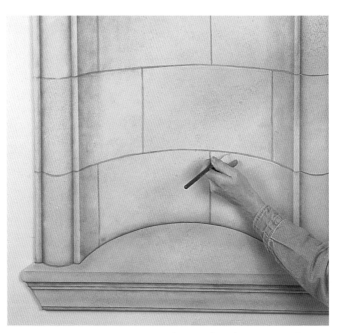

13 The grout lines are painted by hand with a no. 4 round. Thin Medium Gray about 1:1 with extender and follow pattern lines. Some slight variation of line width is okay. Notice how the horizontal lines curve in relation to the eye level, which falls midpoint on the third block from the bottom. The closer the lines are to eye level, the more they seem to straighten out. Above eye level, they appear to curve upward. Below, they curve downward, with the arc becoming more pronounced as the lines get farther away.

14 You can add further detail to the grout lines by painting a thin highlight with thinned French Vanilla along the top edge of the blocks using a no. 4 pointed round brush.

15 Use a paper proof of the stencil design you plan to place in your niche to determine the best placement. The visual depth of this pot must appear to be accommodated by the visual depth of the niche shelf. If it is placed too far back it will appear to be squished in; too far forward, and it may look like it is ready to fall out. It is also very important to your illusion that the object you place in the niche appears to be viewed from the same perspective as the shelf itself, and the perspective of the base of this particular pot works nicely.

16 Each overlay of the pot is first basecoated with Country Twill to completely cover the previously painted grout lines. Dark Gray then covers that, but in a way that is not completely smooth and even, to add to the rustic look of the pot. Use a small artist's sponge to add texture with slightly thinned Metallic Antique Copper. As always, change the direction and pressure of your hand to create a random, nonrepetitive look. Complete all overlays of the design in this same manner.

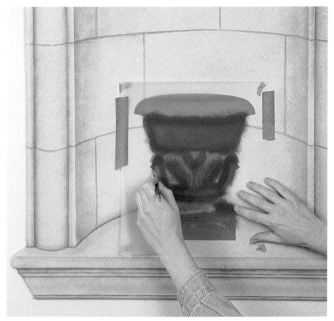

17 Soften the texture on each overlay now by stenciling over the entire surface lightly with Dark Gray.

18 Use Licorice and a ⅜" (1cm) stencil brush to add shading and Glazed Carrots to create highlights, creating contrast and definition between the various elements of the design. Note: The detailed stenciling of this same pot is demonstrated in chapter two.

19 Again, I have used a stenciled proof on tracing paper to help me predetermine design placement. I wanted to use this bromeliad design, but its size is slightly too large for the niche, so the proof allows me to see where I need to make some adjustments and alterations, and that I need to push the design down farther into the pot. Some leaves will also need to be eliminated or shortened.

20 Carefully placed pieces of tape are used to easily redefine the shapes of the leaves. Basecoat all leaves with Italian Sage. It may take two to three thin layers of paint to completely cover the darker grout lines that are behind. Use a hair dryer to speed things along.

21 Shade with a mixture of Olive Green–Dapple Gray. Use Wrought Iron for the deepest shading on the leaves and flower head, which is painted with Glazed Carrots and Barnyard Red.

22 Mix a very thin wash of Medium Gray, and add hand-painted shadows with the no. 8 round brush, mimicking the shape of the leaves and flower on the limestone surface behind. Note: The farther away from the surface object is, the more the shadow will be thrown from it. Consequently, the shadows of the back leaves are painted much closer to them than the shadows of the leaves that are positioned more forward in the design.

23 Add a dark painted shadow extending from the pot along the shelf and up the back wall of the niche. Notice how the shadow itself changes direction where the two planes of the surface meet. Add some more weight to the pot by also shading slightly just along the underneath edge.

ROMANTIC WINDOW

Windows give us a sense of connection to the outside world while expanding our living spaces and our view. Maybe you have a wall or room that is lacking in architectural interest or seems to be closing in on you.

Create this idyllic sunny scene to turn any room into a room with a view. The best part is that you can change your view easily, because this mural is painted on stretched artist's canvas, which can be easily moved from wall to wall, room to room, and house to house.

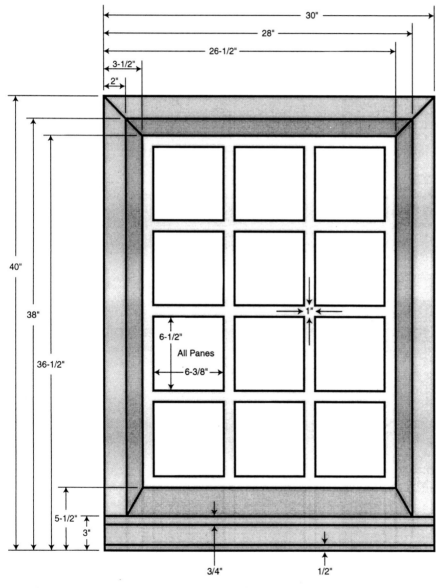

(See Skyscape instructions beginning on page 106 for specific colors and painting techniques used for the sky and clouds.)

SUPPLIES NEEDED

Stencils and Patterns

- Lovely Little Lace and Sweetheart Ivy Topiary stencils from Royal Design Studio
- Twisted Fabric Border and Fabric Drop stencils from The Mad Stencilist
- patterns for cypress and foliage on page 157

Paints and Glazes

- Benjamin Moore Flat Interior Latex
  Decorator's White
  Harbor Fog
- FolkArt acrylics
  Berry Wine (topiary)
  Buttercrunch (landscape and topiary)
  Butter Pecan (landscape)
  Dapple Gray (landscape)
  Dark Gray (landscape)
  French Vanilla (curtains)
  Gray Green (landscape)
  Gray Plum (landscape)
  Honeycomb (landscape)
  Italian Sage (landscape)
  Light Gray (window frame)
  Medium Gray (window frame and curtains)
  Olive Green (topiary)
  Pink (topiary)
  Spring Green (landscape and topiary)
  Teddy Bear Tan (topiary)
  Thicket (landscape)
  Whipped Berry (curtains)
  Wicker White (curtains and topiary)
  Wintergreen (topiary)
- FolkArt Extender
- AquaGlaze

Brushes

- assorted stencil brushes
- no. 8 round
- no.6 filbert
- no. 3 script liner

Miscellaneous

- prestretched artist's canvas: 30" x 40" (76cm x 102cm), ¾" (1cm) thick
- natural sea wool sponge
- clear grid ruler and blue tape
- 4" (10cm) foam roller and tray
- gray watercolor pencil and soft charcoal
- Mylar or E-Z Cut Plastic

1 Using a 4" (10cm) foam roller, basecoat canvas with two coats of flat white latex. Following the measurements on the pattern, use 1" (3cm) tape to divide and define the windowpanes. Tape around the outer edges of the window frame. Burnish well. In order to preserve a clean tape edge for the painting to come, seal the edges of the tape by rolling on an additional layer of white latex, the same color as the basecoat. If there is any seepage under the tape, it will blend completely.

2 Basecoat entire window area with Harbor Fog. Reference the Sky-scape instructions and materials on pages 106–108 to create a soft cloud scene down to the horizon line. Use soft charcoal to sketch in the basic shapes of the landscape.

3 Painting from the background to the foreground, use thinned acrylic paints to slowly build up layers of washed color. Using a stiff filbert brush allows you to scrub in the color, and painting in a horizontal motion will add movement to your landscape. Begin with the Gray Plum in the farthest background, blending into Gray Green, Italian Sage, and Dapple Gray. Use the brighter Spring Green as you come into the foreground.

4 The path is painted with the same filbert brush using washes of But-ter Pecan and Honeycomb. Using a lot of variety in the depth of color will aid in creating a soft impressionistic effect. Avoid painting flatly, with solid blocks of color. Add some of the green colors into the path and vice versa to create unity, flow and interest in the landscape.

5 Small cypress tree stencils provide an easy way to paint in distant trees quickly (you may cut your own from the provided pattern on page 157). Use a variety of gray/greens to stencil in a stand of trees along the horizon line, overlapping them slightly.

6 You can create some filler foliage in the landscape by stippling in some scrubby bushes with a ¾" (2cm) stencil brush. To create depth, work from dark to light. I first stippled in a combination of Thicket–Dapple Gray and highlighted the top edges of the bushes with Spring Green to create some simple but effective shapes.

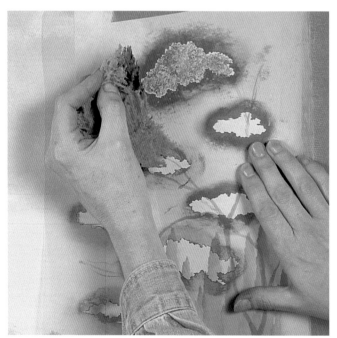

7 Thin Dark Gray and lightly paint in the branch shapes using a no. 4 artist's round brush.

8 In order to create a lacy leaf effect, use a sea wool sponge loaded with paint to sponge through tree foliage stencils. Vary the sizes and shapes of the foliage stencils, and again, work from dark to light colors (Dapple Gray, Thicket and then Spring Green) to create depth. Be sure to overlay some of the foliage stencils to create a nice dense effect. Lastly, sponge some Buttercrunch on the top edges of the foliage to create highlights.

9 After all of the scene painting has been completed, remove the blue tape. The areas that have been protected by the tape are now ready to be transformed into dimensional frames for the windowpanes with some well-placed shadows and highlights.

10 Use your grid ruler to mark a ¼" (6mm) line around the edges of all the squares. Draw miter lines connecting the corners of the inner and outer squares. Also transfer all of the lines from the pattern for the outer detailing of the frame, shelf and molding. Use a gray watercolor pencil to create the lines. When painting, the color will dissolve and blend slightly with the shading and overpainting.

11 Thin Light Gray with water, and lightly paint all the inside areas of the window frames.

12 Use tape to shield the outer corner, and a piece of paper, acetate or Mylar (you will need something with a perfect 90° angle) to protect the inside corner before stenciling the top and left side of the frame with Medium Gray. Notice the angled tape in the upper right and lower left, which protects and defines the mitered corners.

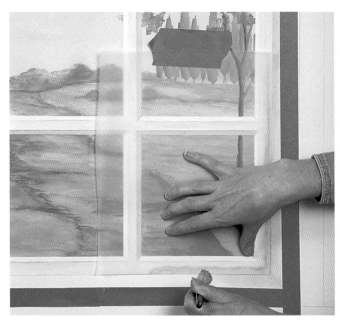

13 The dominant light source chosen for this mural is coming from outside, at upper left. This would create shadows angled away from it that fall inside the room onto the window casing. The lower right areas of the molding that surrounds each small pane were left the original white, which now creates a highlight. Use tape and Mylar to define the cast shadow from the window onto the inner casing of the window. Stencil with Medium Gray. Keep this light and uniform.

14 Use tape again to define the cast shadows (using Medium Gray) from the inner frames of the window onto the ledge and casing. Make sure that these shadows end at the edge of the ledge

15 The window scene is shown with completed shading, all done with tape and the stenciling/shading techniques outlined in previous projects. You could easily stop at this point and have a very believable window illusion. The depth of the canvas casts a real shadow on the wall, emphasizing the illusion. If desired, though, you can continue to decorate your window to match the room it will hang in.

17 To create a delicate lace pattern, stencil a small-scale, overall design (such as Lovely Little Lace), using Wicker White again. The pattern is stenciled with the swag stencil still in place. For each section of the swag, angle the pattern of the lace in a slightly different direction for a more realistic, natural look. Shade and define the folds of the fabric with Whipped Berry. Add Medium Gray to the deepest parts of the folds for more depth.

16 I decided to further dress my window using the Twisted Fabric Border stencil from the Mad Stencilist. The first step is to define the folds of the fabric by stenciling with Wicker White that has been thinned with extender or glaze medium. You want this to be sheer, not opaque! Concentrate more color around the edges, though, to give them some depth and dimension. This stencil design was just slightly too large for this window, so I have adjusted it to fit by taping off on the left side.

Here is the completed window with the addition of a lace drape on the side. At this point you could stop and have a sweet and lovely view. The windowsill provides ample room, however, for additional painting possibilities. A stack of books with some reading glasses, a vase of fresh-picked flowers and a sleeping feline are a few ideas that come to mind. I chose to stencil a sweetheart rose topiary, in keeping with the romantic theme.

18 This topiary is a free-form design. Because the leaves and rose buds are individual and hand-placed, you can easily create a topiary of any configuration, size or shape. It is just a matter of deciding then defining the shape and building it. In this case, the pot was based in first with French Vanilla for positioning, and the basic form of the topiary was sketched in lightly with soft charcoal. I chose to create a ball shape, but you can choose open circles or hearts, cones, double balls or spirals. The background leaves are placed first using Olive Green. This goes quickly. Just use the various leaves, turned in all different directions, to block in the form.

19 To fill in further and create more mass, go back with a dry brush and the same color and fill in between the open spaces of the leaves.

20 Use a lighter color, in this case Spring Green, to solidly layer some more forward leaves on top and in between the first layer of leaves.

21 Position the roses, spreading them throughout the topiary so that they are balanced and facing different directions. Paint the rosebuds solidly with Pink and shade with Berry Wine using a ⅜" (1cm) stencil brush.

22 Finish off the pot by building up a solid layer of Buttercrunch, deepened in tone with Yellow Ochre and shaded with Teddy Bear Tan. Add some of the yellow, Buttercrunch, to the top layer of leaves and the roses to highlight them and bring them visually forward.

23 To carry the yellow color throughout the composition and to add more contrast, sponge some of the Buttercrunch into the foliage of the tree in the foreground.

24 Free-form ivy leaves are used as some filler at the bottom of the pot. These also help to soften the harsh lines of the pot and to bring in some more green toward the bottom of the composition. Different colors of green are used to further define these different types of leaves. With a ¾" (2cm) stencil brush, basecoat the leaves with Spring Green. Use a small ⅜" (1cm) stencil brush to add the darker Wintergreen in the centers of the leaves.

25 In order to make the leaves pop out, trim the edges with Wicker White, using a ⅜" (1cm) brush and "hugging" the edge of the stencil so that just a small portion of the brush is allowed into the stencil "window."

26 The shadow from the window frame is no longer applicable with the placement of the pot, so it is painted out with the background color, Decorator's White. Stipple the color over the area to be covered with a 1" (3cm) stencil brush.

27 An alternative to hand-painting cast shadows is to stencil them. With free-form stencils such as these, the most difficult part is to go back and match up the individual stencils with the leaf shapes. You will be rewarded with a nice clean stencil print of a shadow that is easily executed. For those of you anxious about hand-painting, this is a good substitution. Remember that shadows are only cast on *objects*, so don't have shadows falling on thin air. Use thinned Medium Gray and stencil just to the edge where the previously stenciled leaf begins, not around the whole perimeter of the cutout.

29 Lastly, with a no. 8 round brush, paint in the shadow from the pot onto the windowsill, falling away from the light source in the same direction as the shadows from the window frames.

28 In the case of free-form, you will of course still have to hand-paint in the vines using a no. 3 script liner. Make these vine shadows relate to the leaf in the same way as the original stenciling.

BY-THE-SEA

Wouldn't it be great to have a getaway vacation home to go to? A place where you could spend the morning leisurely wandering the beach and searching for shells and then come home and put your feet up while you listen to the sounds of seagulls and pounding waves, with the smell of salt air drifting through an open window on the summer breeze. Oh well, you can dream about it!

Or you can paint it. Here is another movable mural on pre-stretched artist's canvas, a relaxing coastal scene in muted colors. I have tried to incorporate a variety of painting techniques, that, as always, can be copied and/or adapted in any number of ways. An important addition and lesson here, though, is how to create open windows using simple two-point perspective.

While some of the stencil companies who provided designs for use in this book offer precut stencils for open windows and doors, none of them was exactly the right size and configuration for this project on 36" x 48" (90cm 1.2m) canvas, so I decided to design my own. I have always had an irrational fear of perspective, thinking it must be very complicated (and besides, dealing with numbers generally gives me an artist's headache). I called on Andrea and Richard Tober of A Matter of Perception to help me plot out the steps involved in creating my own windows with tape. Well, anything is easy when you know how! All that is really required to create these perspectively correct windows is some patience and some accurate measuring. Even better, you can follow these same simple steps to create windows and French doors of any size and dimension.

SUPPLIES NEEDED

Stencils and Patterns

- Three Shells and Large Shell stencils from The Mad Stencilist
- Hinges stencil from L.A. Stencilworks
- The Nubble stencil from Red Lion Stencils
- Seagulls stencil from Deesigns
- pattern on page 156

Paints and Glazes

- Benjamin Moore Flat Interior Latex
    Autumn Bronze
    Harbor Fog
    Valley Forge Brown

(See Skyscape instructions beginning on page 106 for specific colors and painting techniques used for the sky and clouds.)

- FolkArt acrylics
    Barnwood (window)
    Blueberry Pie (water)
    Bluegrass (landscape and lighthouse)
    Buttercrunch (shells, seagulls)
    Clay Bisque (window)
    Country Twill (landscape, lighthouse, shells)
    Dapple Gray (landscape and lighthouse)
    Dark Gray (window and seagulls)
    Honeycomb (landscape)
    Icy White (window)
    Medium Gray (lighthouse, shells, seagulls)
    Metallic Antique Gold (window)
    Mushroom (shells)
    Robin's Egg (landscape)
    Slate Blue (water, shells, seagulls)
    Spring Green (landscape)
    Sweetheart Pink (shells)
    Ultramarine Blue (water)
    Valley Forge Brown (window)
    Wicker White (shells and seagulls)
- FolkArt Extender
- Golden's Matte Gel Medium

Brushes

- assorted stencil brushes
- no. 8 filbert
- no. 1 liner
- 2" (5cm) chip brush
- higher-quality 2" (5cm) or 3" (8cm) nylon brush

Miscellaneous

- prestretched artist's canvas: 36" x 48" (90cm x 1.2m), ¾" (2cm) thick
- blue tape
- soft charcoal
- cotton swabs
- string
- clear grid ruler
- palette or foam plates
- terry towel or washcloth

1 To begin, measure in and mark 3" (8cm) from the top and sides, and 5" (13cm) from the bottom of the canvas. Run tape on the outside of the lines to define the window scene area. Basecoat the entire area with a flat sheen of Harbor Fog. Sketch in the basic shapes of the landscape and paint the sky according to the technique outlined on pages 106–109, ending at the horizon line. Note how the cloud formations become smaller and closer together at the horizon line, indicating their greater distance from the viewer. Place the water paint colors out on a palette and thin with water.

2 Using a lot of water in a no. 8 filbert, apply the colors in long horizontal strokes. Begin with the deepest color, Ultramarine Blue, at the horizon line. When you get to the middle ground area of water, switch to Blueberry Pie, and then Slate Blue for the shallowest portion of the water. Be sure to blend the transition areas well with a wet brush.

3 While the washes of color are still wet, go back and create some whitecaps by pulling a damp cotton swab through paint here and there in horizontal lines. Roll the cotton swab between your fingers as you drag it and vary your pressure to create a realistic, irregular shape.

4 After sketching some lines with soft charcoal, basecoat the masses of land using
thinned washes of the landscape colors (Spring
Green, Bluegrass, Robin's Egg and Dapple
Gray), again using long, horizontal strokes.
Add variety and interest to the terrain by layering various washes of color over each other.
The layering of colors adds more richness and
depth. Predetermine where the stenciled lighthouse scene will fall on the peninsula in the
background and leave that area unpainted.

5 Stencil the lighthouse scene using the recommended colors on the
supply list or the colors of your choice. Because it is in the background, it is important to use colors and values that are closely related.
Using sharp contrasts of values and intense colors would visually bring the
painting to the forefront.

6 Note from this detail of the completed stenciling that the rocks and
rolling landscape that the building sit on are part of the stencil, but
additional hand-painting has been added to the cliff area that goes down
to meet the water.

7 In the foreground, a meandering path that recedes into space (a common element in murals), was painted in to help create more movement and depth. It is always nice to break up the masses of land with some foliage. In this case, some clumps of sea grass are painted using the edge of the same no. 8 filbert brush used to paint in the background, but you could easily use a pointed round brush as well. Vary the size and shape of the clumps, the colors used and the length of your brushstrokes for a more natural look.

8 Use a small round brush to paint the flower heads as shown with Honeycomb. Again, variety in the height and size will aid in a more natural look. It is very easy to fall into patterns of repetition, so try to be aware of that and consciously avoid it.

9 Stencil a group of flying seagulls, using the colors listed in the supplies, paying careful attention to placement. Notice that the medium bird is placed with a focus in toward the center of the scene. The reverse would have led the viewer's eye out of the picture. Notice also that one of the smaller gulls is placed near the horizon line, aiding in the sense of distance.

10 Once the distant scene is complete, remove the tape and reposition to shield the edge of the scene and expose the frame of the window. Burnish the edges, and basecoat with two coats of Valley Forge Brown. Allow to dry.

11 For this step, use chip brushes and the layered-dry brush technique outlined under Distressed Painted Wood on pages 70–71. Thin the acrylic paint 1:1 with water and apply in layers using Barnwood first, then Dark Gray, finishing with Clay Bisque. The next picture shows how the grain follows the direction of the wood. Miter the corners by taping off the adjoining areas as you come to the corners.

12 Create a perspective grid following the steps outlined on page 105, and by referring to the illustration on page 156. Use a light-colored watercolor pencil, which is easily removed with a damp cloth when finished. Mark an X on your drawn arc to indicate the open position of the doors.

13 Run a string from the starting point (bottom left corner of window) straight across the X and extending to vanishing point right, which is the point where the string eventually crosses the horizon line (not shown in picture). Be sure to mark that point (VPR). Determine the angle of the top of the window frame by running the string from the beginning edge (indicated on the pattern) to the same vanishing point.

14 Use a level to draw a plumb line from the bottom right edge of the open window straight up to where it connects with the top right edge. Note how the revealed edge of the open window is drawn in on the bottom left. This indicates the thickness of the window frame, which is exposed because the window is opening away from the viewer. Repeat the same process for the window on the right side, referring to both the pattern and perspective illustrations.

15 Run blue tape around the perimeter of all the drawn edges of the window frames and burnish well. As an added precaution against having any paint seep under the edges of the tape and spoiling both the clean edge and the previously painted landscape, you may seal the edges of the tape. Use gel medium and apply two thin coats (allowing to dry thoroughly between coats) with a no. 8 filbert along the edge of the tape that will be painted.

16 Use a foam brush or roller to base-paint in the window frame color Valley Forge Brown. Two to three coats may be needed to cover the painted landscape. Apply the painted texture to the window frame in the same manner as the outer frame, taping off to define where the strips of wood abut in the corners.

17 Use a grid ruler to mark a ¼" (6mm) line at the top, bottom and inside edges of the inner frame of the windows. This will indicate the depth of the inside of the window frame that holds the glass. You will not see this area on the outer edges of the frames because of the position of the open windows.

18 Tape off on both sides and use Dark Gray to solidly stencil a shadow in the areas that are along the top and sides. Use Clay Bisque to stencil a highlight along the bottom of the inside edge. Also refer to step 21, which shows the mitering of this inner corner and the addition of a lighter shadow (optional) on the bottom right window. This is done while the tape is still in place and is a lighter application of the Dark Gray. It is the shadow created by the left edge of the window frame when the light source is coming from the upper left of the picture.

19 To shade and define the inner edge of the window frame, tape off on either edge. Use tape to also shield the corners of the windows that overlap the frame. Shade with a solid application of Dark Gray on the underneath portion of the window frame, using a piece of tape or shield held in place at the mitered corner to define the edge.

20 Stencil/shade down the sides using the same Dark Gray but with a lighter pressure to create a lighter value. Note: If you have trouble controlling the value with an adjustment of pressure, you can thin the color with extender to make it more translucent.

21 This picture shows the completed shading pattern. Notice that the inside edge of the bottom ledge of the window has been defined with a slight change in values. A piece of tape was run across the line horizontally and shading added below.

To set the hinges, measure down 6" (15cm) from the top and bottom edges of the corners of the window frame to indicate the position of the hinges. Paint these by stenciling with Metallic Antique Gold and shading with Dark Gray. Notice how the angle of the hinges changes from the top hinges to the bottom. This is accomplished by simply turning the hinge upside down, so that the angles of the hinges are perspectively correct.

22 Add details to the hinges with a liner brush and Dark Gray. Line the outer edges of the screws to add definition. Add a straight line across to indicate a groove for the screwdriver. Place the grooves at different angles for variety. Circular lines were added on the hinge pins.

23 To create the frosted look of the windowpanes, tape off around the outer edges and apply Icy White that has been thinned with two parts water using a good-quality nylon bristle brush. Soften immediately with a towel, but allow some areas to show streaks.

24 Complete the scene by adding some pretty stenciled seashells in the foreground on the windowsill. There may be ridges of built-up paint along the edges of the window frame where it was taped. Sand these down lightly so that the ridges don't show through on your stenciled shells.

25 Base in the solid shapes of the shells with Wicker White. It will require several coats to cover completely. Be patient! Use thin layers to avoid run-unders. The shells are colored with varying combinations of Buttercrunch, Sweetheart Pink and Country Twill. Darker accents are Mushroom and Slate Blue. Deepest shading is Medium Gray.

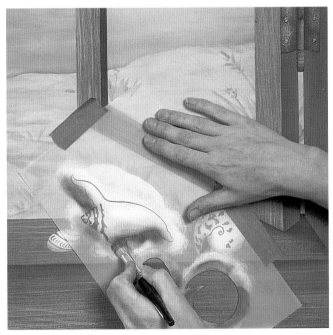

26 Notice that the colors and shading used on the foreground shells is much more intense and shows greater contrast that the colors and shading used in the background scene. This sharper focus of the foreground elements versus the soft focus of the background helps to create a believable sense of distance and depth.

27 Add cast shadows from the shells onto the top surface of the ledge using thinned Dark Gray. Notice that the shadows fall away from the outside light source and echo the shapes of the objects that are creating them.

GALLERY

Following is a selection of stenciled trompe l'oeil murals by various artists and stencil designers that is sure to inspire your imagination. The variety of different artistic and painting styles highlights the many creative possibilities that can be brought into play when designing and planning a stenciled mural.

These murals were created by decorative artist Peggy Eisenberg for a California Showcase House in a mud room, which was the back entrance to the house. The stencils she used are from Deesigns.

GOLF SCENE

A golf scene, complete with trompe l'oeil clubs, painted in a closed area provides a backdrop for the real thing. To the right, a perspectively correct shelf mural on canvas that contains items that relate to the potting area was affixed to an old freezer door.

Artist: Peggy Eisenberg
Photographer: John Cannon

POTTING AREA

The "potting area" skillfully combines both illusionary and real objects (note the stack of painted pots "resting" on the table behind the real ones and the trompe l'oeil seed packets "tacked" to the wall).

Artist: Peggy Eisenberg
Photographer: John Cannon

These two large murals were completed using a "projection stenciling" method that was developed and perfected by the artists. Large sheets of freezer paper are affixed to the wall surface and the mural scene is then "projected" onto it. The stencil is created on site by cutting away those portions of the design that are to be painted. This technique is excellent for large, simple graphic elements, where a precut stencil would be awkward and expensive, and is outlined in the book Projection Stenciling by Linda Buckingham and Leslie Bird.

ARBOR

Notice how effectively the use of some simple perspective and a subdued background expand the feeling of space in this room. Projection stenciling was used to create the large architectural features and background trees. Foreground details were added with a variety of free-form stencils from Buckingham Stencils, and they serve to create movement and soften the architecture while bringing focus and color to the foreground.

Artist: Linda Buckingham
Photographer: Lionel Trudell

GREEK ISLE SCENE

This simple and serene mural creates impact through the use of interesting shapes and angles and the dramatic red tile roofs which punctuate the otherwise cool and soothing color scheme. The look is uncluttered and sophisticated.

The large, angular shapes of the buildings here are easily created and cut using the projection stenciling method. You can employ this technique for creating architectural elements of any size, shape or style. Save postcards, travel photos, calendar scenes and the like for your own resource for future mural scene possibilities.

Artist: Linda Buckingham and Leslie Bird
Photographer: Lionel Trudell

These two whimsical murals were created by talented airbrush artist and stencil designer Sheri Hoeger, "The Mad Stencilist."

"BUNNY" THE DONKEY

The subject of this mural was first photographed by the artist at a State Fair, after she was drawn to his charm and personality. Working front to back, the artist used templates and shields to paint the donkey first, and then stenciled the background "behind" him.

Artist: Sheri Hoeger

Photographer: Dave Adams

GARDEN MURAL *Below*

This sweet scene was created to be the focal point on a nursery wall. The soft colors and shading create a serene feeling while adding color and interest to an otherwise blank wall.

Artist: Sheri Hoeger

Photographer: Dave Adams

FREE-FLOWING GARDEN MURAL

Not all murals need to be contained to one area, or even one wall! In addition to being the entryway to a home, this area also leads to a home office for a financial consultant. A fun, uplifting atmosphere was created with this garden in the hallway to relieve the tension/anxiety that often occurs when making decisions about money.

To create an even more personal statement, each family member took part in choosing elements for the mural and stenciling small portions of it. The rest was up to artist P.J.Tetreault who used custom designs from her collection of precut stencils. The result is whimsical, but the attention to color and shading as well as shadowing makes these elements come to life with the illusion of dimension and depth.

Artist: P.J.Tetreault

Photographer: Skip Dickstein

COUNTRY SCENE DINING ROOM

Stencil designer and artist P.J. Tetreault created this custom mural, which covers all four walls and envelops this dining room in nostalgic comfort. The scene depicts life in the 1700s around the time that the home that is featured in this view was built. Working from photographs, the artist designed stencils depicting both the former and current homes of the family, a hunt scene, flying Canadian geese, and even the family dog to create a very personal and significant work of art that can be enjoyed and appreciated as a family heirloom.

Artist: P.J.Tetreault

Photographer: Skip Dickstein

pedestal pattern for marble finish

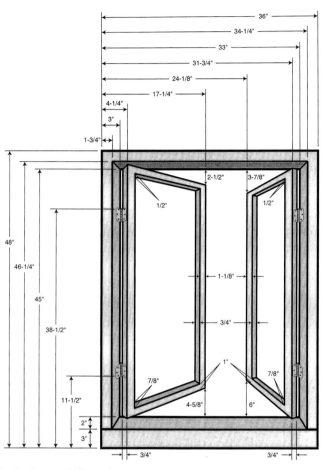

By-the-Sea mural dimensions

cypress and foliage stencil patterns for
Romantic Window mural

RESOURCES

SUGGESTED BOOKS

The Art of Faux by Pierre Finkelstein. Watson-Guptill, 1997.

Basic Perspective Drawing, a Visual Approach by J. Montague. John Wiley and Sons, 1998.

Basic Perspective for Artists by Keith West. Watson-Guptill, 1995.

Grand Illusions: Contemporary Interior Murals by Caroline Cass. Phaidon Press Ltd., 1988.

The Handbook of Painted Decoration by Yannick Guegan with Roger LePuil. W.W. Norton and Company, 1996.

Marvelous Murals You Can Paint by Gary Lord and David Schmidt. North Light Books, 2000.

Painting Murals by Patricia Seligman. North Light Books, 1988.

Projection Stenciling by L. Buckingham and L. Bird. Hartley and Marks Publishers, Inc., 1999.

Stenciling Techniques by Jane Gauss. Watson-Guptill Publications, 1995.

Stencilling on a Grand Scale by Sandra Buckingham. Firefly Books, 1997.

Trompe L'oeil: Creating Decorative Illusions with Paint by Roberta Gordon-Smith. North Light Books 1997.

Trompe L'oeil: Murals and Decorative Wall Painting by Lynette Wrigley. Rizzoli, 1997.

PERSPECTIVE

A Matter of Perception
Andrea and Richard Tober
6748 Hunter Rd.
Elkridge, MD 21075
(410) 379-5112
www.aperception.com
specializing in practical "perspectives" education for artists and designers; offers trompe l'oeil studio classes, travel teaching, multimedia CD-ROMs, and instructional videos.

STENCIL SOURCES

Many of the products and tools used in this book are available at your local home or hardware store. Additionally, many of the stencils, glazing mediums and supplies are available through:

Royal Design Studio
2504 Transportation Ave., Suite H
National City, CA 91950
(800) 747-9767
www.royaldesignstudio.com

Instruction in the art of stenciling is available from Royal Design Studio in the form of a complete video series, as well as workshops held at the San Diego School of Decorative Arts.

Additional stencil designs, artwork and materials were graciously provided by:

Decorative Accents by Peggy Eisenberg
13936 Skyline Blvd.
Woodside, CA 94062
(650) 851-7110

Deesigns, LD.
P.O. Box 960
Newnan, GA 30264
(800) 783-6245
www.deesigns.com

L.A. Stencilworks
16115 Vanowen St.
Van Nuys, CA 91406
(877) 989-0262
www.lastencil.com

LakeArts
P.O. Box 1285
Flowery Branch, GA 30542
(888) 464-2787
lakearts@aol.com
www.lakearts.com
source for PolyMural canvas, artist's canvas, floorcloth and other art supplies

The Mad Stencilist
P.O. Box 5497
El Dorado Hills, CA 95762
(888) 882-6232
www.madstencilist.com

Muracles by Jeff Raum
4950 Moorpark Rd.
Moorpark, CA 93021-2211
(310) 789-4449

Natures Vignettes, Inc.
205 West Meeker Street
Kent, WA 98032
(877) 813-2593
www.naturesvignettes.com

P.J.'s Decorative Stencils!
Box 5774
Albany, NY 12205
(518) 438-8020
PJTstencil@aol.com
source for E-Z Cut Plastic and stencil burners

Red Lion Stencils
1232 First NH Turnpike
Northwood, NH 03261
(877) 942-5466
www.redlionstencils.com

The Stencil Artisans League, Inc.

An international non-profit organization dedicated to the promotion and preservation of the art of stenciling and related decorative painting.

Stencil Artisans League, Inc.
526 King Street, Suite 423
Alexandria, VA 22314-3143
(703) 518-4375
www.sali.org

INDEX